Puzzlemaster

and Gospel Writer

A Handbook for

the Gospel of Mark

by Charles Dillman, PhD

Puzzlemaster and Gospel Writer
A Handbook for the Gospel of Mark
ISBN 978-0-9882246-1-2

© DoubleSixpence Press 2014

DoubleSixpence is an imprint of Treetop Publishing Co.

doublesixpence@gmail.com

This book is dedicated to my wife, Marie Dillman.
I am constantly in awe of her mind, her heart, and her soul.

This book is a result of teaching courses in Biblical Studies at Spring Arbor University over thirty fruitful years.

Spring Arbor, Michigan 49283

Contents

Preface	1
Chapter 1 Mark's Puzzling Beginning	6
Chapter 2 Mark's Abrupt Ending	9
Chapter 3 Why So Little of Jesus' Life?	14
Chapter 4 The Ultimate Question: Who Is He?	18
Chapter 5 The Challenge of Opponents	23
Chapter 6 From Challenge to Open Opposition	33
Chapter 7 The Reader has Inside Information	35
Chapter 8 Peter: Disciple and Apostle	41
Chapter 9 Were the Disciples Really That Slow?	52
Chapter 10 Amazement, Awe, and Wonder	77
Chapter 11 Son of Man: Jesus' Favorite Title	83
Chapter 12 The Key Verse in Mark	120
Chapter 13 Miracles	125
Chapter 14 Parables	164
Chapter 15 Mark's 'Sandwiches'	181
Chapter 16 Can Mark's Gospel Be Outlined?	189
Chapter 17 Final Questions and Issues	204
Some of the Puzzling Things in Mark	224

Preface

WHAT QUESTIONS WOULD WE LIKE TO ASK MARK?

Sometimes when I read a book, any kind of book, I wish I had the writer near-by so I could ask him or her to give me a bit of explanation on parts of the writing. Often I find some parts that aren't fully explained, or places where the writer has something in mind but doesn't give me the "back-story." *If I just had one more clue,* I say to myself, *I could get a lot more out of this.*

There are some times that it is careless writing on the part of an author that leaves me wondering. Sometimes the writer just assumes that the readers know all that stuff. Often it is that there is a great distance in time between the writing and the reading. That's especially true for everyone when we read the writings of Ben Franklin, Thomas Jefferson, or John Wesley, who lived at the same time in the 1700's.

The same thing is true of books of the Bible, filled with timeless truth but coming from a generation eight times further away from us in time than Franklin, Jefferson, or Wesley.

"I try to read the Bible, but I just can't get anything out of it," some people say. To a person who cares deeply about the Bible and who also cares deeply about people, that's a very discouraging thing to hear. It's even worse when the same person says, "Sure, it's easy for you -- you've been to seminary," (or "you've spent years studying it"). There is no good answer for that -- not any that you can make people believe, at any rate. Yet I continue to stubbornly believe that anyone who wants to *can* read the Bible with understanding.

You may remember the old joke about two young boys who saw their grandmother reading her Bible for an hour or more at a time, twice a day --
"Why does she read the Bible all the time?"
"I think she's cramming for her finals."

A grandmother can understand the Bible -- if she'll spend time with it. So can a teenager. But a casual leafing through isn't likely to be enough. And once in a while checking some word or idea in a Bible Dictionary can help a lot. This book is full of observations about Mark's Gospel, and can be a sort of guidebook.

So here is my effort to give the world a test case. The Gospel according to Mark: shortest of the four Gospels, the earliest too, most people believe. But Mark is also the most puzzling. This wasn't careless writing on his part, the unanswered questions and puzzles are included by design. Mark was a very careful writer; I feel sure that's why God chose him to leave for us this introduction to

Christ. But Mark loved puzzles. It was just the way he thought -- it was a gift -- and the Lord can use any of us with whatever gifts we have.

This book is not a commentary. It is an extended series of questions that I put to the writer, Mark. I've asked him questions about the disciples, about Jesus, about the people who opposed him and those who followed. I've also asked about some difficult parts of Mark's Gospel. With a little imagination you can listen in on an interview between Mark and me.

A note about how to follow the discussion: I'm the **Questioner**, and **Mark** gives the answers. In his answers Mark rarely will make any reference to other Gospel accounts, for obvious reasons. When he wrote, none of the other three Gospels existed. Since his writing preceded the others, it would be unfair to hold him accountable for information he doesn't have, but others included.

Mark wasn't among the twelve disciples, but then neither was Luke. That doesn't mean that they didn't have reliable information to write. Strong early testimony tells us that Mark traveled with the Apostle Peter, and had the task of translating for Peter, who could speak Greek, the language of the Roman Empire. Peter's use of Greek was not fluent.

Mark's almost seems like the forgotten Gospel, for several reasons. The first reason is that over 90% of his verses are represented in Matthew and Luke. Second, Mark's is by far the shortest of the Gospels. Third, Mark likes to leave us with puzzles for us to figure out. Many of the things he says purposely in a puzzling way are included in Matthew with the puzzle softened, or even explained.

As you read this book you will find many references to specific passages in Mark. When this is the case the reference will just give the chapter and verse, not the name of the book ("3:12," not "Mark 3:12").

Quotations from the Bible are most often from the English Standard Version, sometimes from another version that happened to be near-by as I wrote, and occasionally it will be a fresh translation (by me) from the Greek.

If you can see yourself as a learner traveling in Mark along with me, welcome. We're not going to challenge the concept of Biblical Inspiration and the Bible's authority -- I fully believe in it, and recommend it. And we never challenge Mark the writer by suggesting that we know better than he did how he should have written it. But I'm going to assume that the questions that I have and that I want to ask Mark to explain represent the kind of questions you would have, too. So in this study we are going to come up with a short list of questions we wish he would answer. You may have some further questions to add, but these are the suggestions I have.

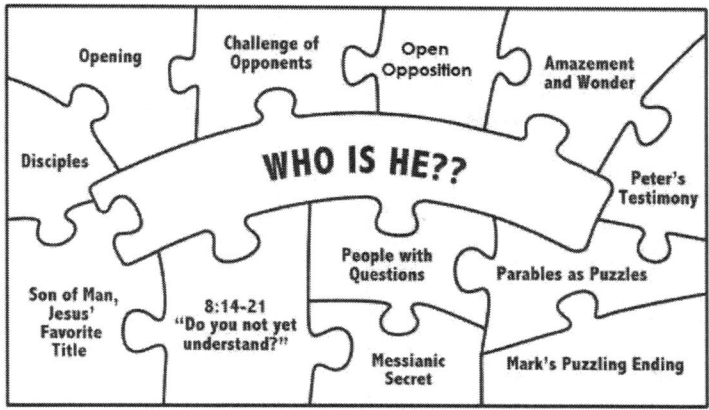

The jigsaw puzzle idea came from watching Mark's Gospel account as it drew readers and students in on one theme after another, then left them to ponder on the information and its setting, without giving them easy answers.

Once you realize that Mark is careful in crafting his writing, and that nothing is out of place or accidental then you can enter into a mental dialogue with the writer. Yes, of course he wrote under scriptural inspiration, but this didn't overrule his natural talents and tendencies. Just as God can use his language skills and vocabulary so also He can use the writer's other characteristics and talents.

Chapter 1

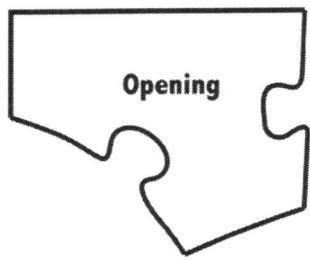

Why doesn't Mark give Background Information about Jesus?

Questioner: Mark, why did you begin so abruptly, with Jesus already about thirty years old, and just ready to begin his public ministry?

At the very beginning of your account you introduce John the Baptist, and immediately move to his baptism of Jesus as an adult. Why didn't you include any of the back-story about Jesus? The account by John takes us back beyond human history, virtually to the beginning of time. Matthew and Luke both report the stories of Jesus' birth and family, even genealogical lists connecting him to many earlier generations. But your Gospel account has none of this, though later on you do include the mention of Jesus' sisters, and of his mother and brothers by name.

Mark: When I began writing, I had never seen a Gospel. In fact, no one had. This is the first of its kind, so of course I wrote about the Savior from what was in my heart, added to what I learned over time from Peter and other trusted preachers and apostles, and the small amount of information that I myself had gained from being a bystander, seeing for myself a very small segment of Jesus' ministry.

From this knowledge base I've written in a way that I can best call *directed*, or maybe *inspired*. But even shaped, as it seemed to me, by the Spirit of the Father above, I had nothing to offer of Jesus' background, family, or childhood.

And of course I want to remind you that a Gospel (or even "the beginning of the Gospel," as I've labeled it) isn't the same as a biography. In a biography it may be important to tell what the ideas and influences were that developed into concepts and motivations in a person's life.

In my case, though, my knowledge about Jesus' life came from sermons and stories used in preaching. That was the preaching and teaching of Simon Peter. Peter knew Greek, of course, as any Galilean did, as a second language; but it was a rough, halting sort of Greek, so he invited me to travel with him as a "communications assistant," to do some translating for him, as he felt the need.

So keep in mind that this information comes mainly from sermons. With the sermon setting in mind, you shouldn't think it too strange that background accounts of Jesus' life: his childhood, or even his early vocation as a carpenter might not be included. Even more strange for my writing would be his ancestry -- though another writer, with slightly different purposes might include an entire genealogy.

Chapter 2

Mark's Puzzling Ending (your own conclusions)

Why is there Disagreement about the End of this Gospel?

Questioner: Mark, what were you trying to convey with the very unusual ending to your writing? According to our best skills in tracing what you actually wrote (and where you ended your writing), for the first hundred years after its writing the Gospel ended with 16:8. Those eight verses tell of the women who came to the tomb, and saw "a young man dressed in a white robe" who told them that Jesus had risen from the dead. He told them to go and tell the apostles -- *and Peter* -- that he had risen, as he said he would. But instead of reporting any more of their story, the Gospel ended with this strange sentence: "they fled from the tomb and said nothing to anyone; for they were afraid." It seems to many people that you ended your Gospel there.

The twelve verses that follow are an attempt, a righteous attempt, by someone much later to fill in the rest of the story. They dip into Matthew, Luke,

9

John, and even include a bit of flavor from the Book of Acts, in order to tell more of the story. The words used and the style of the writing are drastically different from the rest of your Gospel, Mark. We can see this difference in English translations, but in Greek this difference is even more striking.

So, Mark, on the chance that you completed your writing with 16:8, with the words "for they were afraid," why would you end it there?

Mark: Ah, here's a worthwhile puzzle to challenge some of my readers. No doubt you've noticed something about the way I write: I do love puzzles. Often I give all the information that would be needed, much like a person who likes math might give the numbers in a list to be added, but simply does not give the sum, or the bottom line. You'll often find it that way in my writing. I didn't do this to be clever, nor to tease. More about my reason in a moment. But first, I'll answer your question.

When I knew that any thinking reader had enough information to be able to put faith in Christ the Savior, I didn't feel the need to add more details. Jesus had clearly predicted to his followers that *he would suffer and be put to death*; but he didn't stop at that. On three separate occasions he made this prediction and added that "after three days he will rise." Even as Jesus and three of his disciples were descending from the top of the mountain where he had been *transfigured*, he cautioned them not to tell anyone what they had seen until he had been raised from the dead.

So the theme of the resurrection had been firmly planted -- by Jesus -- in the thinking of his followers, and recorded in my written Gospel. So I didn't need to write further, instead trusting my readers either to know the rest of the story, or to be able to supply it.

And, of course, that's exactly what happened. Nearly a hundred years after I wrote, some earnest believer wrote out a composite account of events and teachings following the morning of the empty tomb as he or she believed it should be. I have little argument to make about that attempt, for two good reasons: first, if *this* unknown person had not composed an attempted conclusion, *someone else* would have.

And second, in fact, several other attempts do exist, some of them stemming from two hundred years after the time of the original writing. Scholars have even given them names: "the Freer logion" and "the shorter ending" But now this longer summary is notable and for the most part not a problem, since most of it is drawn from other gospel accounts: Luke, John, Matthew, and a little bit from familiarity with the Book of Acts.

The only objection I have to the additional conclusion, added by someone else, is an unfortunate reference to poisonous serpents and deadly poisons. The poison and serpent assertions are serious problems. They are not supported by any part of the inspired Scripture, and in addition there have been regular reports of people who have tested these assertions in action as an act of faith, and numbers of them have died as a result.

But your question was about why I would have ended the Gospel account at the end of 16:8, with the phrases, [the women] "fled from the tomb; for trembling and astonishment had come upon them; and they said nothing to anyone, for they were afraid."

If it seems odd to you that the account would end in this way, think about these questions:

- Was there more to tell?

- What do you suppose happened?

- Was Jesus really raised from the dead?

- Later, did these frightened women *ever* tell about their early visit to the tomb?

You know the correct answer to all these questions, of course. Even if you had no other Gospel accounts wouldn't you have known everything you would need to know about the resurrection? I think you would. And if so, the answer is *your own* in a way it might not be if I had given you the answer in my writing. Maybe more importantly, I think you've become a genuine participant in the events. As you read it without the addition of later endings, can't you almost feel the emotions of the women? And then don't you almost put yourself in the place of Peter or some of the other disciples -- wanting to hear what the women could tell them, if only they weren't so overcome with fear?

In summary, just one more thing -- even though it isn't included at the end where you expected it to be, the resurrection of Jesus is far from absent in my account. I've already mentioned that Jesus predicted his resurrection in his earlier predictions of suffering and death. It appears in quotations of the words of the Lord himself on five separate occasions in four chapters. (8:31, 9:9, 9:31, 10:33-34, and 14:28) And don't forget too that the final word about the resurrection came to the women by a mysterious "young man dressed in a white robe." Surely you've rightly guessed what sort of "young man" that was, haven't you?

Chapter 3

Why does so little of Jesus' life appear in Mark?

Questioner: Mark, you've made perfectly clear that your writing is not intended to be a full biography of Jesus' life -- aside from leaving out family, birth, infancy, and youth stories entirely, a generous count of the events and incidents of Jesus' life and ministry comes to only something like thirty-one to thirty-nine days* in Jesus' life. If Jesus' ministry was three or three and one-half years long, the full count would amount to between 1,095 and 1,278 days. You have included no events from 98% of those days, giving us information from barely 1/50th of those days. What were the reasons for this severe limitation? Was more information not available to you? Was the length of your work limited by the amount of papyrus available to you? Or was there some other reason, and we readers should keep digging to see if we can discover it?

[The count is that of the questioner, and the variance here is a bit subjective. Wherever I could reasonably suppose that a new scene or episode also signaled a new day, one was counted. There is room for some disagreement. My own variance between

14

31 days and 39 days takes into account a reference to Mark 8:2. "...they have been with me now *three days* and have nothing to eat." and to 9:2, "and *after six days* Jesus took with him Peter and James and John ...."

Mark gives us no record of events during the time references to the three and the six days, but if I include them, I come up with 39 days; without them, 31. When we add the 40 days of Jesus' temptation, we have a reasonable total of 79 days represented. But keep in mind that we have no description of any event for 48 of those days (40 days of temptation, 3 days the multitude was with him, and 6 days between 9:1 and 9:2), so in Mark we are back to 31 days in the life of Jesus.]

Mark: Right -- but the short answer is, I did not write a chronicle, a journal, or a history. You might think about my writing as an extension of the sort of teaching and preaching done by the apostles and other early witnesses. Peter, for example used to tell the stories of the perfect blend of Jesus' teaching along with the commanding way that he dealt with sickness, demons, and other obstacles to ordinary living. Actually, as my writing developed, I myself was amazed at how things fitted together. You have obviously read the writing -- but did you notice that I deliberately did not write down any more specific examples of a repeated event? I give a sample of a wondrous act, but then when Jesus later did something similar (and he did this often), I summarize. Here is just one example of that:

5:24b-34 A large crowd was following him, and thronging about him.

And there was a woman who had had a discharge of blood for twelve years, and who had suffered much under many physicians, and had spent all that she had, and was no better but rather grew worse. She had heard the reports about Jesus and came up behind him in the crowd and touched his garment. For she said, "If I touch even his garments, I will be made well." And immediately the flow of blood dried up, and she felt in her body that she was healed of her disease.

And Jesus, perceiving in himself that power had gone out from him, immediately turned about in the crowd and said, "Who touched my garments?"

And his disciples said to him, "You see the crowd pressing around you, and yet you say, 'Who touched me?' " And he looked around to see who had done it.

But the woman, knowing what had happened to her, came in fear and trembling and fell down before him and told him the whole truth. And he said to her, "Daughter, your faith has made you well; go in peace, and be healed of your disease."

So that's the story: it gives a sample of a person who was healed by merely making contact with his garment. And so that the readers won't conclude that this happened only once, here from a later time is a collected summary statement that shows that similar things happened often:

> Mark 6:56 And <u>wherever</u> he came, in <u>villages, cities, or countryside,</u> they laid the sick in the marketplaces and implored him that they might touch even the fringe of his garment. And <u>as many as touched it</u> were made well.

So, you can watch for summaries and fill them out with more detail in your own minds. My own goal isn't to tell you everything Jesus did, or how he grew up, or who his family was but my purpose is to introduce you to Jesus, the Gospel he came to declare, and to give you evidence for believing.

Chapter 4

The Ultimate Question -- Who Is Jesus?

Questioner: Mark, for twenty centuries Christians have been agreed in their belief that Jesus was the Messiah, and the Son of God. John's Gospel makes it especially clear that Jesus acknowledged being Son of God, and particularly we can see it in the exact words of Christ himself: "I and the Father are One," "I have come down from the Father, and I go back to the Father," and even "For God so loved the world that he gave his only Son...."

You yourself give some testimony to the truth of Jesus as unique Son of God, but seem nearly to conceal it by giving it very little prominence, folding it into other events so that the truth of Christ's son-ship with God the Father does not seem to most readers as prominent, therefore not as important in Mark as in other gospel accounts. Why does it seem so to us? Or are we wrong, and are we almost missing your point?

Mark: If you've looked for references to the relationship of Jesus to the Father, I'm sure that you've noticed that in my account none of the disciples ever calls Jesus the Son of God. But your surprise at this may not seem so striking when you reflect on who *does* call him Son of God.

-God-

For example, you do find this affirmation in the voice of God -- twice. The first time is at the baptism of Jesus and then a second time on the mountain where Jesus was transfigured: "This is my beloved son, listen to him." (1:11, 9:7)

-Demons-

In addition three times there is the testimony of the enemy, in the voices of *unclean spirits,* or demonic beings. (1:24, 3:11, 5:7) I'd wager that you would not normally be inclined to accept the word or testimony of demons. But their credibility rises to astronomical heights when *their* word agrees with that of *God Himself.* Wouldn't you agree?

-Jesus Himself-

It is only slightly more indirect, but still unmistakable, that Jesus Himself refers to his being the Son of God. Again, as with the voice of God this happens twice. The former of those is in 12:1-10, the parable of the vineyard and the tenants. In a story reminiscent of a story about God's vineyard (in the fifth chapter of the Book of

Isaiah), Jesus teaches with a parable about a man who planted a vineyard and rented it out to tenants. The man made every provision for the vineyard, with a protective fence, winepress, and tower. Then he rented it out to tenants who were obligated to care for the vineyard and pay their rent with a share in what it produced.

He sent a number of servants to collect a portion of the produce of the vineyard, but the tenants got away with brutality, time after time. Finally the owner sent his own beloved son -- note the same exact terms that the voice of God used at the baptism and the transfiguration -- beloved son. "Surely they will honor my son."

It is clear that as Jesus tells this parable, God is the owner; the servants are prophets of Israel, the tenants are the politicized leaders of the nation in Jesus' time ("they perceived that he had told the parable against them"). And Jesus, the Christ, is the beloved son.

The second of the two references in his own words to his being the son of God is even simpler and plainer. At the trial before the Jewish Council, which begins in 14:53, the planned plot is not progressing well for the opponents of Jesus because the false witnesses came up with stories that did not agree, so finally the high priest himself asked directly, "Are you the Christ, the son of the Blessed?" Jesus began his response with the simple words, "I am."

Mark continues: So there we have seven references that affirm Jesus' identity as the son of God: two from the audible voice of God Himself, three in the voices of unclean spirits, and two from Jesus himself. What more could we want?

-A Roman Centurion-

Well, fortunately, if we want something more we have it from a man of authority, a man who stood watch over him as he was dying, and who upon the death of Jesus said, "Truly this man was son of God." That witness has very high credentials that provide world-class credibility in the political, imperial, administrative realm: he was the centurion at the cross. He was not a mere soldier, he was a commissioned officer, a leader of men, a captain in Caesar's imperial forces.

-The Writer-

Oh -- and you shouldn't let this one other affirmation of Jesus as Son of God slip past you: it is in the title of my writing, placed there with a purpose. The title is "The Beginning of the Gospel of Jesus Christ, Son of God." It stands there as the seed-bed of the writing. It is not even a sentence, merely a subject -- but it is also the viewpoint and the starting point of the work that I believe came with the help and inspiration of the Holy Spirit.

Questioner: So I guess I could summarize by saying that we have a well-rounded group of witnesses to the fact that Jesus was the Son of God:

> God -- twice
>
> demons -- three times
>
> Jesus -- twice
>
> a Centurion
>
> and, Mark, you yourself.

So instead of your being silent about Jesus being the Son of God, you have given us quite a significant witness list!

Note to the reader: Maybe you noticed that the puzzle piece titled *Who Is He?* is central to the puzzle diagram. It is an over-arching theme in Mark's Gospel. It will come back again, especially in the section on *the Son of Man*.

Chapter 5

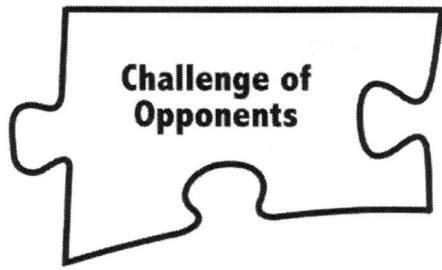

Some People and Groups Watched for Excuses to Turn Against Jesus

Questioner: Mark, as you write about Jesus your very first chapter is filled with a whirlwind of his unbroken success. It shows people around Jesus responding enthusiastically to him and to his words and his works, yet from the beginning of the second chapter onward -- with little exception -- people wonder about him or they fully misunderstand him, or even directly oppose him and his ministry. Even the twelve disciples misunderstand, and surely if left to their own devices they would stand in opposition to his purpose. If he was that generally misunderstood, how does the first chapter fit?

Mark: When he began his mission, Jesus did burst on the scene to great acceptance. Because there is no narrative of Jesus' origins, birth, family, it may seem to some readers that his fame in the early

23

days of his public ministry is unexplainable. But step back and look at the tremendous popularity of John the Baptist earlier in chapter one (verses 4 through 8), in which "all the country of Judea, and all the people of Jerusalem" went out to see and hear him "and they were baptized by him."

So first of all it was a time in which great masses of people were eager to go far out of their way to hear the most stern sort of preaching and teaching -- and they were hearing it with great enthusiasm. Add to that the fact that John had given the strongest sort of recommendation for one who was to come after him, and in John's words, he is "mightier than I, the thong of whose sandals I am not worthy to stoop down and untie."

This helps to explain the enthusiastic reception that Jesus received, as the first chapter of my Gospel shows. But true as it was, it was not the entire story. No one should misunderstand what else was beginning to happen. The Scribes were among the very few authorized leaders of the religious life of the people, held in high regard for their specialty. Many of these Scribes come forward, as you see in the second chapter, to challenge Jesus on four key issues vitally important to them.

These issues had to do with ways of keeping religious laws and other pious practices: how to keep the Sabbath, fasting, eating in the home of (or in the company of) people who do not keep the kosher laws. And what is placed first in sequence, in this chapter of challenges was for the scribes the most offensive thing they saw in Jesus -- the idea that Jesus *declared the paralyzed man's sins forgiven*, and then went the next step and directly claimed that he had the *authority* to forgive sins.

Questioner: Jesus was the target of their disapproval, and if I step into their shoes, I can see their point. In their tradition the scribes taught, and the Pharisees believed, that the Messiah was to come to redeem the covenant-people Israel from their oppressors. Along with political independence, he would also bring a God-given prosperity. Further (and perhaps most important), the Messiah would need righteous people in his administration to help him as he ruled on the earth. Who better to fill this role than the Pharisees?

The Pharisees took righteousness to the highest level they could imagine. Beyond the Ten Commandments there were the ordinances, and the Pharisees were very scrupulous in keeping them. Some of them were detailed commands relating, it seems, to every aspect of daily life, from what to do with a bird's nest to what kinds of fiber can be used in articles of clothing. There were, by actual count, 603 written ordinances of this sort written in the first five books of the Bible. Add the Ten Commandments and you have the total of 613 prescribed rules. All of these were high in the consciousness of the Pharisees -- all of this is quite well known.

But now I ask you, Mark, what about these four things in chapter two? For example, is there any place in the 613 laws and ordinances of the Pentateuch that covers the simple practice of plucking the grains of wheat off a stalk on the Sabbath Day and rubbing it in your hand to be able to blow the chaff away?

Mark: The short direct answer is no, there is no such law or ordinance in the Scriptures. There is the one commandment of the Ten that says, "Remember the Sabbath Day to keep it holy." There are many examples in the Scripture of strong admonitions for refraining from work -- or at least from work as usual -- and severe penalties come as a result of disobedience or neglect. The question has always been raised by earnest people, "How do we keep it holy?" The question wasn't answered very specifically in the Scriptures, but it was considered such an important law that the priests and other officials felt that it demanded ever more specific elaboration and many supporting regulations.

The "Traditions of the Elders"

Mark continues: During the few generations before Christ, the idea of the Oral Torah had become an important part of Jewish thought. The legend developed that when God gave the written Law on Mount Sinai, He also taught Moses the Oral

Law (Oral *Torah*). According to this legend, Moses kept this Oral Torah in his own memory, and taught it to Joshua who in turn taught it to the prophets and sages who passed it down through many generations until it finally came to certain scribes who finally committed it to writing. [This actually came about around A.D. 200 -- well over 150 years after the time of Jesus' ministry, and at least 1400 years after the time of Moses.]

What Did Jesus think of the Written Scriptures?

The Oral Law, held by the scribes of Jesus' day to be of equal authority with the Biblical text of the Hebrew Scriptures, was the foundation of the scribes and Pharisees' opposition to Jesus. In many places we can see that Jesus had an immense knowledge of the written Scriptures -- the written revelation of God, and he considered the Scriptures the key to understanding God, the purpose of life, and eternity. Sometimes Jesus stated openly how much the written Scriptures need to be heeded, and that the oral torah (which he calls "your traditions" was often actually harmful to righteous living. (see especially 7:8-13, also Luke 16:29-30)

The *Mishnah* began with definitions and explanations of passages of the Pentateuch, and amplified and explained the written laws, and really serves the purpose of a commentary. Their error was in treating the commentary with more reverence than their Bible. Even this would be given further commentary in the Jerusalem

Talmud (about A.D. 400) and the Babylonian Talmud (about A.D. 600). These all come from 200, 400, and 600 years after the time of Christ's life, but give us some sense of the traditions that were observed.

In the case of the Sabbath law, the Mishnah took one commandment of the Ten Commandments, and elaborated on it, specifying thirty-nine general prohibitions. There were items that must not be used on the Sabbath. There were also items that must not be moved on the sabbath. One of the thirty-nine prohibitions specifically said that no fire may be kindled -- though that stipulation allowed room for debate whether one may add fuel to keep it burning if it is already lighted.

The regulation of "a sabbath day's journey" went through a progress of interpretation over the centuries. In the Scriptures there is no regulation at all regarding a Sabbath-day's journey. In the teaching of the rabbis, at the earliest stage the maximum distance that could be traveled on the Sabbath was a total of two thousand cubits (just short of six-tenths of a mile). The distance was apparently drawn from a reference to the distance the Israelites must keep from the Ark of the Covenant as it led the way for them as they entered the promised land (established from Joshua 3:4-5, which has nothing to do with either a day's journey or the sabbath). Because the restriction seemed inconvenient, later reinterpretation allowed double this distance, and even later it was doubled again, as well as applying it as merely the distance one could travel beyond the edge of the town, while within the town or city there was no restriction at all, so walking around and around or back and forth within the city was permitted.

So you can see the traditional interpretations were fluid from one generation to another. Sometimes they were based closely on the Scriptures, but more often they were not -- yet by the scribes they were elevated to be equal to the authority and status of Biblical revelation. When Jesus disregarded the Jewish traditions, it is just that. He does not violate biblical law, but the scholars' interpretations, the *halakah*, that had been added through several generations leading up to Jesus' time.

However, the scribes did not see it that way. If you asked them which was a better expression of the will of God, the written Scripture or the oral traditions, they would have said "How dare you ask such a question? Both are equal."

Jesus knew better. If he really was the Son of God, he should know. He had to contend with their opinions, and he was clear in his attempt to correct them. He quoted the words of Isaiah, and then commented on them:

> Well did Isaiah prophesy of you hypocrites, as it is written, 'This people honors me with their lips, but

> their heart is far from me; in vain do they worship me, teaching as doctrines the commandments of men.'
> You leave the commandment of God and hold to the tradition of men.
> And he said to them, you have a fine way of rejecting the commandment of God in order to establish your tradition! (7:6-8)

Though there were differing views on a Messiah to come, one of these views held that God's *Messiah would come <u>at the moment that every Israelite was righteous</u>*. The Pharisees were scrupulously righteous in following laws, ordinances, and regulations; and they wanted everyone else to be righteous as well. They defined that righteousness as including these multitudes of regulations. Because the traditions sometimes were in conflict with the Scriptures, Jesus rejected these extras and based his preaching on the Scriptures alone.

According to the Pharisees, when the Messiah comes he will set up a powerful political reign, and he would need to select people to help him administer that rule. "Who better than us?" the Pharisees privately supposed.

It was for this reason that the Pharisees set themselves up to be the guardians of righteous living for all the Jewish people, setting the rules for everyone, *including Jesus.* Jesus fell far short of their standard, and in this one section alone, Jesus failed their challenges in chapter 2 in these ways:

- He did not admonish his disciples to observe the oral law's regulations on Sabbath observance (2:23-28 -- and then he claimed to be Lord of the Sabbath!).

- He did not observe the fasts (2:18-22 -- and, using metaphors about wineskins and patched garments, he made the claim that many of the former ways of thinking and acting were no longer applicable).

- He ate and drank in the company of tax-collectors and other non-religious, non-kosher people (2:14-17 -- and made the claim that these people's need of him overruled his obligation to be religiously separate and ceremonially pure).

- In their estimation he was guilty of blasphemy by making the claim that he had authority to forgive sins (2:1-12 -- and he challenged the scribes with two things, to heal or to forgive, saying "which is easier?" -- when both were impossible for them).

Because of all these things, all plainly set down in chapter two, these scribes concluded that Jesus could not be even a good Israelite, let alone the Messiah. For them --

1. Jesus was not to be trusted

2. He was not to be believed

3. He was leading astray large numbers of people

4. He could not be the Messiah, as some people were claiming for him, because he was "unrighteous" (according to their definition)

5. Because of these examples of unrighteousness even if all other Israelites were perfectly righteous he would by himself keep the Messiah from coming! Keep in mind that their definition of righteousness included those add-ons not found in Scripture.

So in chapter two the scribes and the Pharisees learn just about everything they need to know about Jesus in order to judge him guilty of extreme opposition to their authority over Judaism.

By this time, they're ready to act. The Pharisees, the Sadducees, the Herodians, and all. This now included the chief priests, who were the elite and most powerful group of all. These groups were in constant competition with each other for the lead in the political and religious power in Israel. They wrestled for political power, and in that they weren't above deception, and in the process they often deceived themselves.

They didn't see eye to eye on very many things. But they've made their decision on Jesus: he's got to go. It will take time and stealth, but on the need to be rid of Jesus they are ready to enter into a huge conspiracy. *How can we destroy him?*

Chapter 6

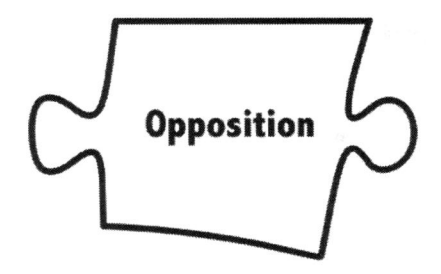

Opposition

The Challenges Result in Open Opposition

Mark continues: Your last question, though, was not only about my chapter 2, it also moves us on into chapter 3, where the questions have been put aside, the fateful conclusion is drawn, and from these leaders, judgment comes forth with a vengeance. There is now open hostility to him and his message. "The Pharisees took counsel with the Herodians how to destroy him."

Questioner: It seems that the hostility of the leading parties toward Jesus begins so very early in your Gospel. Only two chapters and five verses have gone by, and already powerful groups are conspiring together, not to quiet him or to discredit him, but to *destroy* Jesus. Mark, this is only the 78th verse, of your total of 661 verses.

Mark: Well, yes, it is early in the account. But first the challenges and then the direct opposition were the things that Jesus had to contend with nearly all the way through the time of his mission. It was clear that he was not going to have an easy time in accomplishing the will of God among people who were being led by people who were self-righteous and who were not depending on the wisdom and truth of the Word of God. And maybe as you see the difficulties and outright persecution that Christ suffered you may be heartened in any struggles that you may have in life.

Questioner: I notice that you have listed in your third chapter four occasions that show people opposing Jesus: The Pharisee-Herodian conspiracy; scribes who try to interpret his power over demons as from the devil; then his neighbors (some translations say *family*); then his mother and his brothers. Along the way in the same chapter you highlighted Jesus appointing the twelve disciples. Since the theme of this chapter seems to be on opposition to Jesus, isn't this out of place?

Mark: Well, not really. If you look carefully you'll see that the last of the disciples to be listed was "Judas Iscariot, *who betrayed him*." Jesus wasn't safe from opposition among people he knew well, including neighbors and people he called to serve with him in the mission. Even his own mother and brothers misunderstood his purpose and methods.

Chapter 7

The Reader Has Inside Information

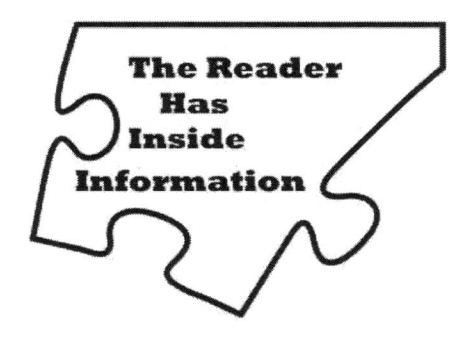

The reason the Reader has greater knowledge

Questioner: Mark, will you tell us why the people around Jesus have less information or less perception than we do as we read this Gospel?

Mark: There's a very simple reason for this -- that's the way it really was. When Jesus came as a man in Israel, and when people looked at him, no matter how closely they looked they could not see a halo. Unlike the pictorial representations of him by artists through many centuries, he didn't always have feet clean and free of the dust of Israel's roads, nor did he have pristinely-clean garments with no sweat stains. With the exception of the one time when his form was transfigured (9:2-8) there was no aura, no glow, no halo. There were no obvious marks of his identity, nothing about his appearance that set him apart. In fact, I could say the most surprising thing about Jesus may be that he looked so unsurprising.

Though I did meet him, I didn't know him well during the time of his ministry. I knew him best through the word-descriptions and introductions Peter made of Christ as he proclaimed him in place after place as we traveled together. Peter had spent a lot of time with Jesus, and was with him not just as one of the group of twelve, but often as part of a closer group of three. They were together as disciples of the Master for a little over three years, so he knew him very well. I learned most about Jesus in the countless hours of travel and in the many occasions of being careful to listen closely to Peter's descriptions -- but I myself heard Jesus in Jerusalem, and even on the night of his Last Supper, as I helped to serve at the Passover meal.

Questioner: Mark, as we read your Gospel account, we feel that we can sense pretty clearly what is going on in the action you have described. But as we, almost like an audience watch this dramatic action taking place, we see that many of the ordinary people who are involved in the action itself are not very perceptive. They miss the point, or they don't understand what Jesus has said, or they don't comprehend its significance. How can they be so insensitive to God at work through

Christ? It is almost as though there were no clues for them to see, that would reveal who Jesus really is.

Mark: If you've noticed, my writing gives you (and actually all the readers), some special "insider" information, that the people around Jesus didn't have. The first example of this is there right at the beginning -- in the first verse of chapter one. The reader gets the benefit of seeing the title that I put on the writing: "*The beginning of the Gospel of Jesus Christ, Son of God.*" None of the people around Jesus would have known that at any early stage, but any reader, even a very humble one, would have better information than the people who were there, observing the action.

Following immediately after the title, the readers see the quotation of two notable passages from the Scriptures -- with reference to the ministry of John the Baptist, who served God as the one who prepares the way for Jesus.

Then the reader has the testimony of John, "*After me comes one who is mightier than I... he will baptize you with the Holy Spirit,*" pointing to the "mightier" ministry of the one who came next, Jesus. Then this testimony is followed not merely by the baptism of Jesus, but also by the voice of God from heaven, "You are my beloved son..." Here again this is given as "insider" information, for it is a voice to Jesus and not to John or the crowd of people nearby. So Jesus gets to hear it -- and so do the readers.

Questioner: So there, in the small space of eleven verses, there are four separate strong testimonies that in Jesus there is, to put it mildly, much more than meets the eye: we as the readers have that information given to us "on a silver platter," but nobody around Jesus got any of it, not even the message from heaven.

Mark: Right. And if you care to go on further, you will note the special information in verse 12 of the first chapter: *the Spirit* drove him out into the wilderness for a time of temptation. A casual observer seeing Jesus might describe the action, saying merely that Jesus "went away into the wilderness for an extended time before beginning to preach in Galilee." But you, as a reader of this account, get the specific mention that *the Spirit drove him out into the wilderness.* And this is followed in the next verse with the information that "the angels were ministering to him."

So here is the special insider information just at the beginning of my account.

    1. The title

    2. Two prophetic passages from the Old Testament

    3. The words of John the Baptist

    4. The voice of God

5. The Spirit Drove Him Out Into the Wilderness to be Tempted

6. The Angels Ministered to Him

Of these six, only the testimony of John was heard by the bystanders, but the reader gets to be "in the know" on all six of them.

This short list is only a brief sampling of this technique, used to place the reader in a favored position of understanding. There are many places in the writing where the reader is allowed to see things behind the scenes, and therefore the reader becomes a better, more well-informed interpreter of the action than people who appear in the story. Better informed than even the disciples.

Other techniques are incorporated in this Gospel, as well, that give a reader insight that the persons in the action do not have. Let me show you an example from chapter two, in the story of the paralyzed man and the dismantled roof: ". . . Jesus saw their faith . . ." Maybe anyone there, seeing four men taking apart the structure of a house, would conclude that they had strong faith; but not only is it made plain to the reader that they had strong faith, but that Jesus responds to that faith -- not only the faith of the paralyzed man but also explicitly the faith *of those who brought him* to the presence of Jesus. The reader can perceive the dynamics of the situation, particularly as it involves the bearers, the paralytic, and Jesus.

Then the narrative focuses on "some of the scribes ... sitting there, questioning in their hearts." Readers are even more informed on the dynamics, now being handed two questions and a harsh judgment that these scribes were silent about, but were thinking. It is an amazing thing when Jesus is able to perceive what people are thinking. Examples of this are very rare in the Gospels. It is even more rare to find that the writer reveals *to the reader* what people are thinking -- this emphasizes even more the characteristic that I've included, of allowing the reader to have knowledge that the people around Jesus did not have.

If you watch carefully for them, you can find other examples of this characteristic scattered throughout my Gospel writing. Maybe you've noticed that you can see inside the mind and thoughts of the woman who touched the edge of his garment. (5:28-29)

In a later story you can see into the thoughts of both Herod and his wife Herodias. (6:19-20, 26)

In fact, regularly there will be the telling phrases such as "they were afraid," "he was troubled," or even "they were terrified." If you will watch for these glimpses inside the minds of people you'll get a better feel for what's happening.

Chapter 8

Peter: Disciple and Apostle

Mark continues: After Jesus' public ministry was complete, there was a small change that had a great big effect. When the *learners* didn't have their Teacher present with them anymore, they had to take very seriously the other title Jesus had given them. The small change? They stopped thinking of themselves as "disciples," (students), and took up the other title that Christ had given them, that of "apostles" (authorized and empowered representatives). The great big effect? This was not merely that they had a message to share, but that they had a drive, an urgency to give that message. I cannot speak for all of the apostles, but I had the kind of relationship with Peter so that I can tell you what I observed.

Since the time that God raised Jesus from the dead, and ever since the time when Christ ascended to heaven, Peter has been tireless in his efforts to declare to everyone who Jesus is. At first, he thought that because Jesus came as God's Messiah to the Jews, the message should spread quickly through Jewish populations.

   For a while, that is what happened. But then Samaritans received the message -- and even though the Samaritans have some Jewish roots and beliefs, nearly all Jews consider Samaritans very distant from the faith. When the Samaritans proved to be open to the good news of the Messiah, this caused many of us to begin to reconsider our ideas about Christ's mission.

   Then just a bit later when Peter himself was directed to declare the good news to a Gentile Roman centurion named Cornelius, and other Gentiles with him, the larger truth dawned upon him, that God meant for salvation to be proclaimed to everyone.

    It was for that reason that Peter expanded his vision and his outreach, and began to travel to various places with the message. His use of Greek was halting, or as he might say "rough," and so he invited me to travel with him and translate as needed. I counted this a great privilege. Not only did I have the opportunity to get well acquainted with Peter, but through him to meet Jesus in Peter's proclamation over and over, day by day.

After a number of requests, the people of various locations including Rome prevailed on me to write down the essence of Peter's proclamation about the Lord. In this I had the strong sense that I was not only representing the insights of Peter but also that I was acting under the guidance of the Spirit.

The Failings of Peter

Questioner: Mark, what you have just told us about your association with Peter brings up a question I feel I have to ask. You say that your presentation of the Gospel primarily comes from Peter's own words. How can this be? Peter is one of the main characters described in the writing itself. The description of him for the most part is given through his words, and to a lesser extent through his actions... and yet...

And yet, the impression we get of Peter in your writing is very far from flattering. Instead, we see a follower of Jesus who is bold and boisterous, who has an exaggerated vision of his own abilities and an unrealistic concept of what Jesus' plan is. On the one hand Peter wants to protect Jesus from some things that must take place, and on the other hand he wants to push Jesus into doing some things that are out of place.

Mark: Yes, Questioner, you've noticed something that can be a real help in understanding. Very often

Peter jumped into the discussion or into the action without thinking things through with any care. Here is one example: at a momentous point in the narrative, the time of the transfiguration. Peter comes forth with a comment and a plan of action which turns out to be a bad plan; and in my narrative I added simply, *"because he did not know what to say,"* leaving you to make your own conclusion, but the clues are there, and putting it as kindly as we want, we still know that this was the suggestion of a fool, or at least a foolish suggestion.

Peter's Testimony

At another point -- you can notice what happens just *after* Peter comes forth with a perfect testimonial as to the role and identity of Jesus, in contrast to the varied guesses that people were offering.

> Jesus: "Who do you say that I am?"

> Peter: "You are the Messiah (the Christ)."

> Jesus: "The Son of Man will suffer many things and be killed; but will rise again."

Peter: (took Jesus and rebuked him, scolding)

Jesus: "Get behind me, Satan. You are not on the side of God but of man."

Peter's Fall

So in a very short moment of time Peter has gone from the heights of perception and insight, with the implied praise of Peter by Jesus, to the deep dark waters of opposition to God, and the direct condemnation of the Christ.

On the final night of Jesus' earthly life after the Passover supper together with the twelve, Jesus took the inner circle of three disciples, which consisted of Peter, James, and John, to be nearby as he prayed in great earnestness. After a time he approached them but found all three sleeping. The same thing was to happen three times in all, over the period of a few hours. Each time, Jesus tried to impress on them his deep disappointment. The first time, he spoke directly to Peter instead of to all three of them:

> And he came and found them sleeping, and he said to Peter, 'Simon, are you sleeping? Could you not watch one hour? Watch and pray that you may not enter into temptation; the spirit indeed is willing, but the flesh is weak.'

Questioner: I can see that the intensity of Jesus' disappointment is clear from his words to Peter, and it is made sharper in the name he chose to use: "Simon." This is the name used in the first chapter when Simon was first introduced, but in the initial introduction of the entire group of twelve disciples this Gospel says, in 3:16, "He appointed the twelve: Simon (to whom he gave the name Peter) ...."

The new name, meaning "rock," (or "rocky") must have signified some quality that Jesus saw already, or wanted to develop, in this disciple. It's significant that Simon Peter is identified by his name *Simon* six times before 3:16, but after that verse the name that Jesus gave him, *Peter,* is consistently used in this Gospel, 18 times altogether. Except for this one time Jesus never reverts to the earlier name. I think it's a measure of Jesus' disapproval and disappointment in him that he pointedly refuses to address him as Peter at this time. Even so, he came back and found them sleeping twice more.

Peter's Single Greatest Failure

Peter's Fall

Mark: But the most startling failure of Peter is his denial of Jesus. When Jesus was placed under arrest in Gethsemane by "a crowd" of people sent by the chief priests, scribes, and elders, Peter followed along, right into the courtyard of the high priest. As the examination proceeded, Peter remained nearby in the company of the guards, warming himself at the fire. Eventually a young servant girl of the high priest came and confronted him, saying that he had been one of those with Jesus. Peter denied it saying "I don't even know what you're talking about."

Peter's denial of Jesus does not end there, not even when he heard the reminder of Jesus' warning specifically to him. Only hours earlier, just before Jesus and the disciples had left the place where they observed the Passover meal, Jesus had predicted that all of his disciples would abandon him. Peter, bold and impetuous, replied that even if all the others fell away he would not. But Jesus replied that Peter's would be an especially severe abandonment -- three times repeated -- and "this very night," before the rooster crowed twice.

The third denial was accompanied by not only lies but also an oath -- a curse upon himself.

Immediately the rooster crowed for the second time, and with that the full realization of what he had done came upon Peter, and he broke down and wept.

Questioner: We've watched Peter through this sequence of events, and see how he had failed in his best intentions and in his promise. It must have been the most humiliating of his several failures, and not the sort of thing that he would want to be remembered for. Doesn't it seem that the inclusion of this episode is convincing evidence for the idea that some people have, that Peter could not have been any major source for this writing?

Mark: Yes, almost everybody would agree with you. Most people are eager to hide their failures, and hope that they never come to light. But Peter isn't like most people. And in his proclamation of the events in the life of our Lord I've seen him include dramatic descriptions of each of the failures that you have described. Further, I have seen his listeners seem to reach out to him in sympathy, connecting with the man who failed, and also seeing that here was a man who had such self-confidence that it was almost pride. Yet in the telling of his failure the pride was wiped away, and the man stood humble before Christ.

The message was clear. Anyone can try for the best and yet fail; and this failure can still be forgiven and can be overcome. As Peter was given the privilege of continuing to carry the message of

Jesus after failure and forgiveness, so the bright hope dawned in his hearers that past sins and faults and failures do not have to put to death any hope of serving the Lord. Maybe you can sense Peter's own willingness to tell his failure when you read it.

Questioner: Actually, each of the examples of Peter's failures has the mark of Peter's own story. With very little editing of the nouns and pronouns you can see Peter's own public confession. Here are two or three examples: I'll try my hand at putting them as Peter might have said them in his preaching.

> After six days Jesus took me, and James and John, and led us up a high mountain by ourselves. Then he was transfigured before us, and his clothes became radiant, intensely white, as no one on earth could bleach them. And there appeared to the four of us Elijah with Moses, and they were talking with Jesus.
> Then I said to Jesus, "Rabbi, it is a good thing that we're here. Let us make three shelters, one for you and one for Moses and one for Elijah." Frankly, I did not know what to say, because we were terrified. Then a cloud overshadowed us, and a voice came out of the cloud, "This is my beloved Son; listen to him."
> And suddenly, as we looked around, we no longer saw anyone with us but Jesus only. (9:2-8)

Mark: Well done! It sounds a lot like the way Peter used to tell it. I think you've caught the spirit of Peter well. Peter's natural inclination shows itself perfectly here: when he didn't know what to say, he nevertheless said *something*. Often it wasn't the fitting thing at all, just as this example shows. He thought of making three huts, or maybe he had in mind shrines, not really aware that this supernatural experience was temporary. Often Peter jumped into discussions without waiting to understand the role of others, or the standpoint of Jesus.

But of course the low point for Peter was the three times he denied even knowing Jesus (14:66-72). Here the issue was not Peter speaking up too quickly, but the exact opposite. He wished to hide his association with the Lord. This time it was cowardice, and the source of the threat he perceived twice was a young servant girl, and later some ordinary bystanders.

But, in his preaching Peter boldly told of his own failure. In having his weaknesses and failures open for all to see, Peter stands in very good company. Some of the greatest people in the Scriptures, those who seem to stand head and shoulders above the ordinary in being followers of God, also have had their failures -- and yes, sins -- portrayed publicly for all to read.

For example David, king of all Israel, had a time of great sin and guilt with terrible effects in his family and in the entire nation. His sin was not kept hidden, and is even held up in the Scriptures as evil. A significant part of his life was in moral ruin. Yet through it all he is called "a man after God's own heart."

Abraham, the father of us all, had failings on more than one occasion. The Scriptures do not say of him that he was a perfect man, or a perfect follower of God, or even that he was a righteous man. They say that Abraham believed God, and that trust was credited unto him for righteousness. Abraham has the singular distinction of being called "the friend of God."

Similar things could be said about failings of Jacob, Gideon, and many others throughout the trail of history of God's covenant people; and so the Bible has a long tradition of being frank about sin, and forgiveness. Peter stands in that tradition.

As he preached about Christ he told as much about Jesus as possible. The story of Jesus had to include Peter prominently among the disciples, but if he were presented as invariably a hero it would not only be untrue to the facts, it would remove him from being a person the rest of us can identify with. The account we have has the ring of truth.

Chapter 9

Were The Disciples Really That Slow to Understand Jesus?

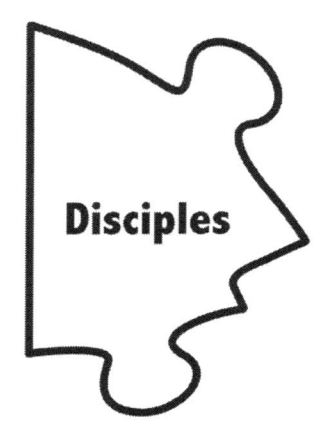

Questioner: Mark, Even though it seems that the disciples were quick to leave everything that they knew including their livelihood, to follow Jesus, yet at several points along the way they seem to misunderstand Jesus, or they seem unable to get tuned in to the real purpose of his ministry. Even after they had been following him for quite a while, he saved them all from the great danger of drowning in stormy seas by commanding the winds and the sea to be calm. Within moments they were saying to one another, "Who then is this that even the wind and the sea obey him?

It's totally clear that their remark to each other is that Jesus is not like ordinary men. But in these circumstances their question "Who then is this?" seems to be a strange response. Who were *they*, to follow him for months, if they had to wonder about this? It makes us wonder *who then* did they *think* they were following? Haven't they seen any clues in all this time that Jesus was not an ordinary man with the ordinary limitations of an ordinary man? And in particular, if he were just the ordinary person, why would they choose to follow him?

When Jesus Walked on the Water

One of the most dramatic series of events in the experience of the disciples came shortly after the disciples had been sent out two by two to represent him in ministry to the people. "So they went out and proclaimed that people should repent. And they cast out many demons and anointed with oil many who were sick and healed them." When they returned from their missionary work, Jesus took them away for a time of rest -- but the crowds of people saw them going by boat, and rushed on foot to their intended retreat location. In his compassion, Jesus began to teach them at great length, and, because of the lateness of the hour, this made it necessary to feed them. So with scant provisions Jesus performed the first feeding of thousands. That evening, just after this miracle, Jesus sent the disciples off in the boat without him.

Storm and wind arose as the disciples began to cross the sea. They were trying to make headway in the boat, but the wind was directly against them. The night was a long one, and morning daylight was still hours away when they saw something. They thought it was a ghost, but he identified himself and spoke to them in comforting words.

> And he got into the boat with them and the wind ceased. And they were utterly astounded, for they did not understand about the loaves, but their hearts were hardened.

The Questioner continues: It had been a day and a night filled with wondrous events, events that could never have been anticipated or expected. Earlier, nobody could have said, "Ho hum -- now I suppose he's going to feed the whole crowd with just this small bag of food." Or later, in the wee hours, there was not a disciple's voice saying, "What time do you suppose he'll show up out here, walking on the sea?" These were astonishing, unexpected, miracles -- miracles that had never happened before, either in the life of Jesus or otherwise.

No matter what else they were, these miraculous events surely show that Jesus has great power over ordinary physical things -- so now my question, Mark, is about the disciples: why was it that the twelve seem so slow to catch on to the fact that seems so obvious, that Jesus is filled with power from above, and his wisdom is not like that of any other person.

The most puzzling part of this episode is when you tie together the fact that the disciples were "utterly astounded" (the Greek word is *existanto*), together with the fact that they did not understand about the loaves, and this was because their hearts were hardened. (6:52) So each thing rests on another: *hard hearts* led to their *failure to understand* the miracle of feeding the 5,000, and this in turn led to their *total astonishment* at Jesus walking on the water.

Then too, Mark, I need to ask what it means when you comment that their hearts were hardened. Maybe I need to change the way I've always thought about that concept. My understanding of the *heart* in the Scriptures is that it normally involves the *will,* so I would think that it was willful stubbornness that clouded their judgment about what they saw. Am I right about this?

Mark: No, Questioner, in spite of the centuries that separate my writing and your own time in history, you've been right on target -- up until now. But here I need to help you figure something out. Remember that once they're written, the words that any writer wrote don't change. Once they're down on papyrus or vellum they're in a fixed form, so it's the reader who has to adapt and try to understand.

There is a very clear way in the Greek language to write about stubbornness, but that wasn't the idea, so I didn't use that expression. If you want to put the right description in other terms you could say "*their minds were insensitive. They weren't open enough to understand the whole truth.*" For some people it might be more understandable to refer to it simply as *closed minds*.

Actually, it was Jesus who brought up this concept, the time they were all in the boat crossing the sea. He warned about the yeast of the Pharisees and of Herod: "Do you not yet perceive or understand? Are your hearts hardened (that is, *are your minds closed and unable to see the real meaning of this*)? (8:17)

It was the same resistance of mind that made his opponents watch Jesus closely to see whether he would heal the man with the withered hand even though it was the sabbath. "And he looked around at them with anger, deeply grieved at their hardened hearts." (3:5)

God was at work. Christ was the focal point on earth of divine action. The disciples were quick to follow him, particularly the first five (Simon, Andrew, James, John, and Levi). In spite of their early enthusiasm, they still questioned how he had such power ("Who then is this, that even wind and sea obey him?"). And, as we've seen, their minds were closed so they couldn't grasp the full meaning and implication of the miracle of the loaves and fishes.

So we shouldn't see the disciples as willfully stubborn, but as having minds closed to the fullness of truth, and therefore unable to understand.

The disciples' response right after He Predicts His Persecution and Death

Questioner: On three separate occasions in the middle section of your Gospel Jesus makes the prediction that tragic events will happen to him shortly:

8:30-31	9:31	10:32b-34
And he strictly charged them to tell no one about him. And he began to teach them that the Son of Man must suffer many things and be rejected by the elders and the chief priests and the scribes and be killed, and after three days rise again.	He was teaching his disciples, saying to them, "The Son of Man is going to be delivered into the hands of men, and they will kill him. And when he is killed, after three days he will rise."	And taking the twelve again, he began to tell them what was to happen to him, saying, "See, we are going up to Jerusalem, and the Son of Man will be delivered over to the chief priests and the scribes, and they will condemn him to death and deliver him over to the Gentiles. And they will mock him and spit on him, and flog him and kill him. And after three days he will rise."

These predictions of his persecution, death, and resurrection are very important -- for Jesus, certainly, and also for you, Mark, as you wrote. But one of the things that we notice as we let the significance roll over us, is that each time the meaning or its importance seems in some way to be lost on the disciples.

If we continue our chart to the next verse in each description we see a pattern.

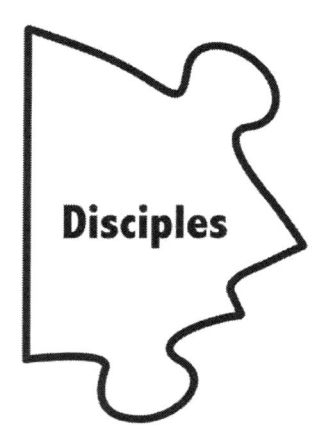

Disciples

8:32-33	Mar 9:32-34	10:35-41
And he said this plainly. And Peter took him aside and began to rebuke him. But turning and seeing his disciples, he rebuked Peter and said, "Get behind me, Satan! For you are not setting your mind on the things of God, but on the things of man."	But they did not understand the saying, and were afraid to ask him. And they came to Capernaum. And when he was in the house he asked them, "What were you discussing on the way?" But they kept silent, for on the way they had argued with one another about who was the greatest.	And James and John, the sons of Zebedee, came up to him and said to him, "Teacher, we want you to do for us whatever we ask of you." And he said to them, "What do you want me to do for you?" And they said to him, "Grant us to sit, one at your right hand and one at your left, in your glory." Jesus said to them, "You do not know what you are asking. Are you able to drink the cup that I drink, or to be baptized with the baptism with which I am baptized?" And they said to him, "We are able." And Jesus said to them, "The cup that I drink you will drink, and with the baptism with which I am baptized, you will be baptized, but to sit at my right hand or at my left is not mine to grant, but it is for those for whom it has been prepared." And when the ten heard it, they began to be indignant at James and John.

Questioner: These three predictions are very similar. They tell us that Jesus was courageous and unflinching in the face of the opposition of the powerful religious authorities and others, and that he was fully aware of the destiny that lay in store for him -- that is, that he was going to be killed. On each of these three occasions, without elaboration or explanation Jesus says, "after three days he [the Son of Man] will rise."

But Mark, my question is still about the disciples. With the ominous nature of this message from Jesus -- undoubtedly to prepare them for the coming situation, why were they so dense as to miss the point so completely? Peter had his turn in 8:32, and seems to come so near to understanding Jesus' meaning. In fact, I'd say he got it, but he didn't like it. He spoiled his perceptiveness by disagreeing with Jesus' message, and actually *rebuking* Jesus. And the rest of that story was that Jesus in turn had to rebuke Peter, telling him sharply that his thoughts weren't in tune with God. So as close as Peter comes to understanding, he receives a pretty harsh evaluation from Jesus.

Then, Mark, when I look at the second time Jesus foretells his persecution and death (9:31), I see disciples who are out of the loop and pretty content in their ignorance. Maybe it went down something like this:

> Andrew: *"Matthew, I didn't get what Jesus meant, that he would be delivered into the*

hands of men. Do you know anything about that?"

Matthew: *"No, I wasn't really paying close attention. I was trying to get these account books to balance. Judas, are you sure there isn't a hole in the money bag?"*

Judas: *"Oh, Matthew, you accountants worry too much about money. I think your business courses didn't do anything but make you nervous. ... And no, I didn't understand what Jesus was trying to say, either. What about some of you other fellows?"*

Thomas: *"Well, I may have been the only one listening, but I confess it seemed like the Teacher is going through a hard time just now. If he's <u>that</u> worried about going to Jerusalem, I think we should just set that plan aside for now. Passover next year might be better in the long run. That way we all could have more time to recruit more followers for the Kingdom movement. The way I figure it, by then we could be the biggest thing in the land -- that is, if we can steer clear of the Romans. What do you think, Peter?"*

Peter: *"I'm going to stay out of this discussion, Thomas. One day last month he talked this way, said almost the same thing. I tried to talk Jesus out of this kind of negative, fatalistic, thinking and he gave me a royal scolding that made me feel so humiliated, and almost made me want to give up on him on the spot! I never told you guys, but he actually called me the devil. 'Get behind me, Satan,' he said. I'll never forget how that made me feel -- won't forget it till the day I die. So, no, just leave me out of this."*

James the son of Alphaeus: *"Well, ... that explains a lot. I had been wondering why you've seemed so quiet recently. Hey, guys, if Peter's going to keep a low profile for now, why don't we elect somebody else to be our spokesman to Jesus. Any nominations? -- besides me, I mean?"*

Thaddaeus: *"Oh come on, James. Do you really see yourself as leadership material? You're a great guy, but you aren't even the number one <u>James</u> in this group. That would be James Bar-zebedee, John's brother. I don't know quite how some have greatness thrust on them, but I'm pretty sure I don't have it. A long time ago I gave up listening for Jesus to say "...and you too this time, Thaddeus," so I could be included among the guys who travel those little side-trips with Jesus, like up on the mountain, or where somebody just died. ... Anyway, if it came to a vote, who would you say is the greatest one of us? Especially if nobody could vote for himself? What do you think, Bartholomew? ..."*

Questioner continues: Mark, you reported in simple terms that the disciples did not understand the saying, "and they were afraid to ask him." But you then wrote that then Jesus asked them what they were discussing along the way, "...but they were silent; for on the way they had been discussing with one another who was the greatest." I've tried to imagine just above, in terms as friendly to the disciples as possible, how that conversation might have taken place. When you reported this, you made the statement without comment, and while you don't report direct disapproval from Jesus, he uses their failure to teach on a very important part of his message.

Mark: Yes, questioner, I think you've got it. One of Jesus' main themes was the principle that in God's way of keeping accounts the first will be last, the last first; greatness is revealed in being a servant; and to receive a child in the name of Christ was to receive the Christ himself.

After the Third Prediction

Mark continues: The third prediction of Jesus' persecution, death, and resurrection is longer and more detailed. Jesus tells of separate stages:

(1) he will be delivered to the chief priests and the scribes

(2) they will condemn him to death

(3) they will then deliver him to the Gentiles

(4) they will mock him

(5) they will spit upon him

(6) they will scourge him

(7) they will kill him

(8) and after three days he will rise.

Questioner: A serious and solemn prediction, anyone would agree. Shocking almost beyond measure. But still focusing on the twelve, what comes next is to me pretty shocking, too, though in a different way.

James and John are brothers, sons of Zebedee, and are two of the inner circle of three disciples of Jesus. Now, with no comment by them on Jesus' prediction, these two approach Jesus with a very strange request: to us it sounds as though they want Jesus to promise to grant them one wish without revealing what it is. He entertains the notion, but first, wisely, he insists on knowing what they want.

What they want is nothing less than power and glory for themselves. Their request is that in some future time, "in your glory," that one of these brothers be positioned right next to Jesus on his right, and the other to have the position next to him on his left. It doesn't escape our notice that this request would completely edge Peter out of the inmost circle.

Under some circumstances, I suppose it should not seem strange that they should ask this. It's a very natural thing for people to want power or fame, or both. But their request came immediately after this third prediction, where Jesus gives such a graphic description of step after step of humiliation and inhuman treatment designed to bring torture and finally death, and these disciples seem completely dense, unaware to the greatest degree.

Maybe James and John failed completely in understanding what Jesus had said -- or maybe they understood it and thought that their own plan could improve the situation somehow. But the shift seems so abrupt, moving from his detailed description of his coming rejection and trial, to his death and resurrection on the one hand -- then suddenly to their ambitious "let's move Peter out" plan. Maybe this request was a continuation of the earlier discussion about who was the greatest.

> ***Zebedee's Wife***: *James and John, I think it's time we had a discussion about something that's been bothering me. I'll bet it bothers you, too -- and I think you ought to say something. I'm very proud that both of you have been so supportive of Jesus' mission, and obviously your Teacher has noticed. From the time you boys were little I've taught you how important it is to present yourselves useful and thoughtful.*

> ***James***: *Well, Mom, we've always tried to ...*

> ***Zebedee's wife***: *Right. And both of you being in the inner circle of three with Jesus is a very high accomplishment. But surely you notice that Peter is an embarrassment to the whole mission. He talks when he should be listening, and he is always saying the most inappropriate things. You two have told me some of them yourselves, and I can just*

imagine what else goes on. So here's what I want you to do. When Jesus sets up his organization to rule the nation, I think that you, James, should be his right-hand man, and John on the other side. Or it can be the other way around, if you like. But the Teacher has only two hands, so that would move Peter just that little bit further away.

I think you two boys should ask for his promise on this, but if you don't want to I could ask for you. Oh, I know -- how about this? You could bring up the subject, and I could just "happen" to be passing by and I could put in a good word for you. Do you think that would work?

Matthew's Gospel includes this episode, adding the detail that the request was initially made by the mother of James and John. Including their mother in the story may cause us to give more thought to a part of our understanding, and consider the possibility that this request was not a spur of the moment idea, but was the result of earlier discussions within the family of Zebedee.

With all the problems implied in the request by James and John, Jesus uses this occasion to teach about humility and serving others. "You know that those who are supposed to rule over the Gentiles lord it over them, and their great men exercise authority over them. But it shall not be so among you; but whoever would be great among you must be your *servant*. And whoever would be first among you must be *slave* of all. For the Son of Man also came not to be served but to serve, and to give his life as a ransom for many." (10:42-45)

Christ sets the standard for his followers. No posing, no exalted position, no high-ness and mighty-ness, no claims of authority. Rather, the posture of a servant. What kind of servant? He piled one word for humble service upon another: a word for service as a fellow-worker, and a word for a servant who works long hours under another's orders. (10:43-44; also 9:35 and 13:34)

Mark, through all of this we've been watching for a defined answer to our question. Were the Twelve actually that slow in their understanding of the teachings of Jesus? Was it that rare that Jesus urged his followers to place others before themselves? He had emphasized the need to be humble very recently, when people were bringing children to him. At the time the disciples were interfering, thinking of Jesus' time, or energies, or the insignificance of the children. Jesus responded with, "Let the children come to me, do not hinder them; for to such belongs the Kingdom of God. Truly, I say to you, whoever does not receive the Kingdom of God like a child shall not enter it." (10:14-15)

Mark: When I felt the prompting to sit down and write about the mission of the Christ, it was never part of my goal (or what I felt that God wanted me to do) to write everything in exactly the order it happened. I think you'll recognize that there are many ways to write about a person's life and goals.

In fact, even though his life was short, with Jesus there were so many things to include, in myself it was hard to feel confident that I had everything where it should be.

Peter's preaching, remember, was my main source for information about Jesus. Like most good preachers he used to suit his preaching to the needs of his hearers. This means that if there were a number of people there who were just new to the gospel he might speak very simply, but if most of the audience were well along in the faith he could speak of some of the more difficult things. We can learn from Peter in both kinds of his preaching.

Mark continues -- The central part of your question was about the twelve, and how difficult it seemed to be for them to be in tune with Jesus and his purposes. Could I suggest that you or I might have been just as slow in understanding?

I mentioned before that where Jesus was concerned, he looked very much like anybody else. No visible halo, no glow -- except during the Transfiguration. (9:2-3) It wasn't easy for anybody to see beyond the obvious. Nearly all the time his appearance was very ordinary. When you see somebody who looks very much like anybody else, it's natural to be amazed if you hear teachings that are far wiser than the ordinary, and especially when the teacher makes a wise reply to a question that was clearly set as a clever trap.

There were a few times when you would have seen with your eyes his majesty in his physical appearance, but those times were pretty rare. I just mentioned the transfiguration, but that happened at the top of the mountain, in the presence of only Peter, James, and John. Only these three disciples were there, so you and I would have missed that. Another time might have been during and after the forty days of his temptation, maybe only at the end when angels came and ministered to him. Even after his resurrection it is said by John in his Gospel that he could easily be mistaken for some ordinary person.

So yes, the disciples were very often short on understanding, but let me explain how that actually may work out God's purposes for our benefit.

- **Why Would the Disciples Follow Him?**

Questioner: If Jesus' appearance was "very ordinary," as you say, then I can't understand the sudden positive response to Jesus from a number of people. For example right at the beginning, we have this short narrative:

> And passing along by the Sea of Galilee, he saw Simon and Andrew the brother of Simon casting a net in the sea; for they were fishermen. And Jesus said to them, "Follow me and I will make you become fishers of men." And immediately they left their nets and followed him. And going on a little farther, he saw James the son of Zebedee

and John his brother, who were in their boat mending the nets. And immediately he called them; and they left their father Zebedee in the boat with the hired servants, and followed him.

The calling of Levi, reported in chapter two, is another example. He was sitting at the tax table, and Jesus simply said "Follow me," and Levi stood up and followed him. I would think that a tax collector, acting in behalf of the governmental (or maybe religious) authorities, would not be free to leave his station with its papers, record books, and currency. But thinking about it I suppose this could have been a tax table with several "stations," and therefore staffed by more than one tax official.

Mark, we can wonder about the men who walked away from their employment another time. But just now I want to ask you about the abruptness of Jesus' calling of these five disciples, and their response. What was it that caused them to just get up without delay and go with him? Of these five, we know very little about their families. We know that Peter had a mother-in-law, though we do not know if he had children, or even if his wife was still alive.

For James and John, we know their father's name, and that he was still active in the fishing business, because when Jesus called them "they left their father in the boat with the hired servants" to follow Jesus. We also know that their mother was an active, assertive woman. We know nothing at all about Levi's family except that he was called a "son of Alphaeus" (and incidentally so was another disciple, the other James).

Questioner: Keeping in mind what you have said about Jesus looking very much like any ordinary man, why would these men, without any dramatic miracle, or even any great words of wisdom, so suddenly drop their occupation, their livelihood, and become full-time followers of Jesus?

Mark: Ah, an excellent question -- and my answer may bring up one or two other things you may have been wondering about. It may seem that this is off the subject for the next minute or so, but it'll become clear to you why I'm giving this information at this point.

You see, there are a number of reasons why my Gospel account shouldn't be too long. First, there was the whole scarcity and cost of writing materials -- one single sheet of papyrus, instead of costing only a few pennies as in your world and your day, in my time it might represent a thousand times as much (think ten dollars or more for one page) in raw materials, skill, and time. You can see that in practical economic terms no document should be longer than necessary.

In addition, I have a fixed belief that the writer should not do all the work. If the writer doesn't report every detail then the readers have the opportunity of figuring out some things for themselves, and they can become participants in the knowledge. They then, in a sense, "own" it as their own. Hold on to that thought, because it may be that as we go on you'll have more questions that relate to this idea.

- **Extra Information From Luke's Account**

Mark continues: Now let me fill you in on what *else* was going on when Jesus first called these men to follow him. I didn't describe for you everything that happened that day. For more of the story, a way to clear up what else was going on, you could look at a passage in the Gospel as recorded by Luke.

> On one occasion, while the crowd was pressing in on him to hear the word of God, he was standing by the lake of Gennesaret, and he saw two boats by the lake, but the fishermen had gone out of them and were washing their nets.
> Getting into one of the boats, which was Simon's, he asked him to put out a little from the land. And he sat down and taught the people from the boat.
> --**Luke 5:1-11**

Luke takes the time to describe the setting. It is already Luke's 5th chapter, but this is where he first mentions the call of any of the disciples, including Simon. There you can read that Jesus invited himself onto Simon's fishing boat, and asked him to push out a little from the shore, so he could teach the large crowd while sitting in the boat. Then his telling of the story continues.

> And when he had finished speaking, he said to Simon, "Put out into the deep and let down your nets for a catch." And Simon answered, "Master, we toiled all night and took nothing! But at your

word I will let down the nets." And when they had done this, they enclosed a large number of fish, and their nets were breaking.

In the boat, first we see Jesus teaching, and then Jesus asked Simon to guide the boat out into deeper waters to let down the nets. For Simon and the others it had been a long unsuccessful night for their fishing partnership. At first, Simon protested, but then with reluctance he agreed to let down the nets. Within moments they had enclosed a huge catch.

> They signaled to their partners in the other boat to come and help them. And they came and filled both the boats, so that they began to sink. But when Simon Peter saw it, he fell down at Jesus' knees, saying, "Depart from me, for I am a sinful man, O Lord." For he and all who were with him were astonished at the catch of fish that they had taken, and so also were James and John, sons of Zebedee, who were partners with Simon. And Jesus said to Simon, "Do not be afraid; from now on you will be catching men."
>
> And when they had brought their boats to land, they left everything and followed him. -- **Luke 5:7-11**

After this dramatic fishing experience, now also involving James and John, Simon himself made a heartfelt gesture, falling down at Jesus' feet and proclaiming himself unworthy of even being in Jesus' presence; but Jesus responded to him with the call, "Do not be afraid; from now on you will be catching men."

So now, in answer to your question, you can see that the whole event has much more to it than I included in my account. These fishermen had heard Jesus' words in the teaching he did from the boat, and right afterward they had the even more vivid testimony of the amazing catch of fish, contrary to the expectation of the seasoned fishermen. On this evidence of Jesus' unique authority and power -- in word and work -- they "left everything and followed him.."

You shouldn't be surprised that I didn't tell the extra details of the story. I gave you clues in my first chapter, when I told you that Jesus' fame spread everywhere throughout all Galilee -- before he even got out of the synagogue. And the action of the part of the first chapter following Jesus' temptation looks like it could have all happened within a week or so. That is, until you see the few little clues that show that it was more likely three months or more. (1:38, 39, 45)

- **Extra Information From John 1**

Questioner: This helps to fill in the picture, and it's also a good reminder for us to continue studying, and comparing the accounts that we have that tell us about Christ.

With this in mind, I should mention that even this was not the disciples' first encounter with Jesus. I've looked into the first chapter of the Gospel as John the son of Zebedee recorded it, and there I see an even earlier occasion of some of these same disciples.

> The next day again John was standing with two of his disciples, and he looked at Jesus as he walked by and

said, "Behold, the Lamb of God!" The two disciples heard him say this, and they followed Jesus. Jesus turned and saw them following and said to them, "What are you seeking?"

And they said to him, "Rabbi" (which means Teacher), "where are you staying?" He said to them, "Come and you will see." So they came and saw where he was staying, and they stayed with him that day, for it was about the tenth hour.

One of the two who heard John speak and followed Jesus was *Andrew, Simon Peter's brother.* He first found his own brother *Simon* and said to him, "We have found the Messiah" (which means Christ). He brought him to Jesus. Jesus looked at him and said, "You are Simon the son of John. You shall be called Cephas" (which means Peter).

The next day Jesus decided to go to Galilee. He found Philip and said to him, "Follow me." Now Philip was from Bethsaida, the city of Andrew and Peter. -- John 1:35-44

So we are introduced to two men who were followers of John the Baptist. The location is Bethany beyond the Jordan, many miles from the place where Jesus called the fishermen Simon, Andrew, James and John to follow him.

It was here, east of the Jordan River where John the Baptist was preaching, that Andrew and his brother Simon were at that time followers of John the Baptist. Simon was soon to be given the Greek nickname *Peter,* meaning "Rocky". As followers of John the Baptist they would listen closely to every word he said, and heard in surprise and joy when their leader pointed them to Jesus as *the Lamb of God.* Without hesitating, they began immediately to follow Jesus.

Summary

Mark: So putting all of this together, it adds depth to the story, doesn't it? Even better, it may help you and other readers to know that (1) there was something so compelling or charismatic about Jesus that some people could quickly make the decision to follow him; (2) there were some people who were able to make that decision (in spite of other commitments, like fishing or tax collecting); and (3) the disciples had a longer time to make up their minds than you might have guessed.

Chapter 10

Why so Much Amazement, Awe, and Wonder?

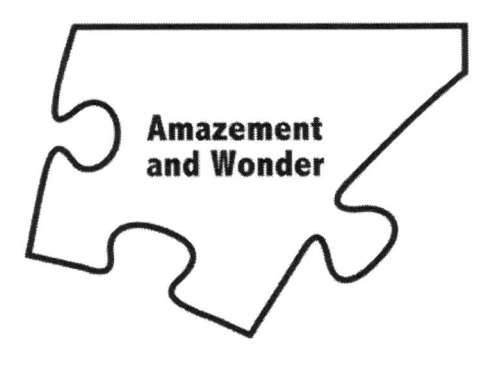

```
Amazement
and Wonder
```

Questioner: This is related to the previous question, but I want to ask about the many times the people in your writing are filled with *amazement, wonder, awe,* or *marveling,* all the way to *astonishment.*

Mark: I'm not surprised that this question would come up. It's an obvious question, and has a pretty easy answer. over twenty times in my writing (ah, but who's counting?) I described people's response to Jesus, his words, and especially his actions with one or more of these words of amazement. In meaning they aren't far apart -- one of these words could often be substituted for another. Any of them refers to a *need for a change in mind* where the actions, or sometimes the words, of Jesus are far different from the expected. You might think of these times as examples of "the unexpected Jesus."

Questioner: So our goal in this record of the Good News is naturally to discover what we can about Jesus the Christ, the Messiah sent from God. And we can never forget the amazing fact that God gave his own testimony about Jesus in so many words: "This is my beloved Son; listen to Him."

If Jesus meets all expectations, that is a wondrous thing. It would be a wonder no matter who did. No one else has done just that: Adam didn't live up to this potential. Nor did Noah. Not Abraham or Gideon, not Moses or Elijah, not even King David. But this is Jesus: he came onto the scene without much fanfare.

Mark: -- Right: he set forth his agenda, and you can find that agenda in one sentence in my writing, in 1:14-15

> Now after John was arrested, Jesus came into Galilee, proclaiming the Gospel of God, and saying, "The time has been fulfilled, and the kingdom of God is just at hand: repent and believe in the gospel."

In his preaching he didn't mention himself: he pointed to the kingdom of God and the good news, the gospel. Yet this message was an alert -- something is coming, just around the corner: be ready!

Israel had a long and interesting history. There were times of prosperity, times of great blessing and the clear approval of God. But just as often the nation called the "chosen people" were in times of discouragement and even despair. When Jesus came the Jewish nation was living in an uneasy truce with powerful imperial forces. The Roman empire had begun an extraordinary expansion by military conquest, making whole nations and kingdoms into adjoining Roman provinces in the empire. They ruled over each of these lands with measures, often ruthless, that were designed to govern effectively, and especially to keep the population from revolt. They kept armed military contingents in each of these provinces as an occupation force.

Though large numbers of the Jewish people longed for freedom from Rome's rule, they knew that they had to be cautious in every way, even in their words, because to speak of, or even hint about revolt was dangerous, and could lead to severe punishment or even to execution. If some entire group were suspected of planning to mount a resistance to Roman rule, harsh measures would immediately be put in place, and word would quickly be sent to Rome.

Both the Pharisees and the Sadducees had their ways of coping with this Roman rule. The *Pharisees*, as we discussed quite a while ago, were a religious and political group of highly trained people who thought of themselves as the most earnest of the Jewish people. They were energetic in trying to live by the Law as found in the books of

Torah, the five books from Genesis through Deuteronomy. And to secure their righteousness even further, they were serious about adhering to the oral teachings, the traditions of the scribes. In the traditions they could sharply distinguish between things permitted and things that were not allowed.

Here's where a problem arose: they not only observed all the restrictions themselves (restrictions that were not in the Scriptures), they stood as guardians of righteousness for the nation. They even had sent priests and Levites to question John the Baptist, investigating his own understanding of his identity and role.

The *Sadducees* were another religious-political group, very different from the Pharisees in many ways. Their interest was not about finer points of the law or the traditions of the elders. Because they did not believe in the resurrection, or even life after death, their focus centered on personal peace, prosperity, and contentment in the present life.

Their greatest concern was that the chosen nation, the Jewish people, must survive, and compromise was the path to survival. Because of the existing Roman domination and power, it was important not to make waves. There was a delicate balance that must not be upset by people or groups who didn't understand. The Sadducees worried about the Pharisees: they thought the Pharisees leaned toward fanaticism. So even more, they would worry about someone like Jesus -- especially when he began to talk about a new "kingdom," and a new reign being very near.

There were other groups of Jews with a varied mix of religion and politics in the days of Jesus: there were the Essenes (who left us the Dead Sea Scrolls), who believed in keeping separate from most of the society; and the Zealots, who longed for armed revolt. Each of these represented a different response to a harsh military occupation. Most of the ordinary people did not actually consider themselves members of any of the formal groups, but they had leanings in one direction or another.

When Jesus began to preach about the kingdom of God it was likely that the Sadducees would think of a political and military movement that would try to compete with the Roman regime.

Sadducees could not imagine such a movement being successful, because the might of imperial Rome would immediately oppose it. If a movement of this kind even *began* to become popular it would give all the excuse that the Romans needed to bring swift and harsh punishment not only on the people who started it and those who became followers, but the violence would spill over onto many innocent Jewish people. When the Sadducees, and the Pharisees along with them, experience surprise at the words and works of Jesus, their almost immediate opposition to him rules out words friendly to his mission.

81

Questioner: But on the other hand, the amazement of the people who heard him and the awe of the people who saw him can help us to see him more clearly, and to know him better. In one sense, when they are amazed we can be amazed along with them, and in the observation we see that the power of Jesus cannot be contained in the natural world. When he causes the paralyzed man to walk, the people around Jesus have to reset their focus from the normal. The easy question, "what is humanly possible?" has to morph into something far higher and less limited, with the better question, "What *else* is possible?"

Mark: The "what else," I'm sure you already understand, is beyond the *humanly* possible. It represents things that only God can do.

I hope my readers, in their minds participating along with the people in my written account, will reset their focus toward the unlimited power that was in Jesus.

Chapter 11

SON OF MAN

Son of Man, Jesus' Favorite Title

Questioner: Mark, we asked before about the title of Jesus as "Son of God," and I appreciated your patient answer when you pointed out that the title is used in all eight times by a total of five witnesses. But something a little related to that comes to my mind just now. There is another title for Jesus in your Gospel, "Son of Man," but only Jesus uses it -- and always as a reference to himself. No one is *ever* recorded calling him by that title. No one ever ran up to him and said, "O Son of Man, come and heal my daughter!"

Thirteen times you quote Jesus using this phrase. There are some people who look at it and wonder exactly what Jesus meant by it.

> 1-- Did it mean only that Jesus was fully human, maybe to correspond as a human counterpart to his title "Son of God," which indicates the fact that he had also fully the nature of God? Then *son of God*, *son of man*, the two sides of his nature?
>
> 2-- If that's so, then did it mark him as being able to have both of these natures, but only one at a time -- so when the title "son of man" was used, his human characteristics would be more prominent?
>
> 3-- Or, as some people have suggested, did Jesus have some <u>other</u> person in mind? They point out that it would seem strange for him to use this awkward formal phrase when it would be easier just to say "I." He certainly had no trouble using the word "I" to refer to himself, because he did so over fifty times in just this one Gospel.
>
> 4-- Or maybe he was merely inventing a strange-sounding title, something to keep people wondering, or guessing ..
>
> 5-- Or, just maybe, these sayings aren't from Jesus at all. Could it be that you, the

writer, invented this phrase and "put words in Jesus' mouth"?

Questioner continues: -- As for me, Mark, I feel sure that Jesus did use the phrase "Son of Man," and I have the feeling that there may be more to it than we usually understand. Could you confirm my feeling -- or correct it, if I'm on the wrong track?

Mark: Well, if we could deal with these five notions in reverse order, let's first look at the suggestion (**5**) that the phrase is one I invented, as the writer or recorder of the action. I think you'll soon see that Jesus meant something very specific in this title. There are some very large truths packed into this simple, puzzling, phrase. Take my word for it that it would be far beyond my simple powers to invent this phrase with all its significance. In addition, if someone believes that I have written about truth but done so falsely, then my writing would be in vain. In the sense that I was a reporter I have reported faithfully what Peter preached about the Savior to his hearers. So no, this was not something I invented.

You asked (**4**) if Jesus was inventing a title for himself to impress people, or just for the effect of making people wonder. That makes me wonder what sort of motivation you think Jesus had in his ministry. Surely you aren't suggesting, are you, that he said or did things trying to keep people off-balance, or to seem more mysterious. I would find it hard to urge people to listen to Jesus on the important things he said, if he was manipulating the attitudes of his hearers on a title, as this question would suggest. But I think this suggestion will be put to rest as I lead you through the other options.

Another suggestion (**3**) was the idea that Jesus used that title to refer not to himself but to some other man. This idea can actually be tested, simply by looking at the passages. They are all, of course, grammatically, in the third person singular.

Actually, I'll easily agree that it would have been easier for him to say "I. " So if he used the longer phrase, let's look for a reason that is good enough.

The first two suggestions try on for size the idea that *Son of Man* identifies, or maybe merely focuses on, the humanity of Christ. He somehow bore the nature of Deity, and at the same time truly took on humanity. How God could do this, even the wisest of scholars still debate. But I'll try to explain why Son of Man does not serve to describe or define his humanity.

Questioner: Mark, I've counted, and noticed that you've quoted thirteen times that Jesus used this phrase, *son of man*. If we look at all thirteen, we soon see that they can't all mean the same thing, even though they refer to the same person. Jesus is always the person, but the phrase may speak of one part of his ministry, or another, or yet another.

The Son of Man: Persecuted, Suffering, Killed, and Vindicated

Mark: The largest group of Son of Man sayings by Jesus make up this category. There are six of these. Let's look at each one of them. Here is the first one, and it follows immediately after the occasion when Jesus asked the disciples to report what people were saying about Jesus, that is "who" were they tying Jesus' identity to. Then, going far beyond these attempts to identify Jesus with one of the men of faith in the past, Peter makes the bold but simple assertion that Jesus is the Christ. It was a commendable declaration, but as often occurs in my Gospel, Jesus strongly charged them to say nothing about him. Immediately then we have this reference that the Son of Man will suffer great persecution at the hands of the chief priests and scribes, and he will be killed, but rise again.

> And he began to teach them that the *Son of Man* must suffer many things and be rejected by the elders and the chief priests and the scribes and be killed, and after three days rise again. -- Mark 8:31

I suppose it's possible that some reader could take Jesus' words as a reference to some other man. The process of human communication is tricky enough that if something *can* ever be misunderstood then at some point it *will be* misunderstood.

The same risk is there for some of the other references --simply because of the grammatical structure used by Jesus ("the Son of Man must ..."). They do not identify who the "Son of Man" is, except to emphasize his suffering, death, and resurrection. Some readers have actually toyed with the idea that Jesus really meant somebody else. But the disciples themselves knew better. In 8:31-32, Peter began to rebuke Jesus, clearly recognizing that Jesus meant *son of man* as a reference to himself.

> And he said this plainly. And Peter took him and began to rebuke him.

The rebuke went both ways, for the next words are these:

> But turning and seeing his disciples, he rebuked Peter, and said, "Get behind me, Satan! For you are not on the side of God, but of men."

Clearly, both the historical setting and the interaction between Jesus and the twelve show that Peter and the others knew that Jesus was referring to himself.

Here are two more times Jesus spoke of his rejection by people and his death, but his resurrection that would surely come.

> And as they were coming down the mountain, he charged them to tell no one what they had seen, until *the Son of Man* had risen from the dead. (9:9) . . . And he said to them, "Elijah does come first to restore all things. And how is it written of *the Son of*

> *Man* that he should suffer many things and be treated with contempt? (9:12)

This pair of references, together, were part of a short conversation Jesus had with the three disciples of his inner circle. Look again and you will see that the main truths emphasized about the Son of Man are his suffering persecution and his vindication in rising from the dead.

There are two more references to notice in this connection, because they have very much the same message as we have just seen. Jesus uses the *Son of Man* title, and he speaks of the Son of Man's persecution, death, and rising again. Scholars like to call the three references in 8:31, 9:31, and 10:32-34 "the three predictions of the passion" (*passion* in the original sense of deep strong feeling or suffering). These are pretty much alike, except that while the first two are not as specific, the final one has a much more detailed and more graphic description than the first two.

> for he was teaching his disciples, saying to them, "*The Son of Man* is going to be delivered into the hands of men, and they will kill him. And when he is killed, after three days he will rise." -- Mark 9:31

> And they were on the road, going up to Jerusalem, and Jesus was walking ahead of them. And they were amazed, and those who followed were afraid. And taking the twelve again, he began to tell them what was to happen to him, saying,

> "See, we are going up to Jerusalem, and *the Son of Man* will be delivered over to the chief priests and the scribes, and they will condemn him to death and deliver him over to the Gentiles. They will mock him and spit upon him and scourge him and kill him. And after three days he will rise. (10:32-34) -- Mark 10:32-33

So far we have seen that each of the three predictions of the passion uses the title *Son of Man* and the first two use the phrase without making it explicit (even though it is clear) that the Son of Man is Jesus. The same thing can be said for the conversation with Peter, James, and John just after the Transfiguration. Then we suddenly see in the final prediction that he began to tell the twelve what was to happen *to him.* (10:32)

The Authoritative Son of Man

Mark continues: When we look for references to Jesus' teaching where it is completely clear that Jesus means himself when he uses the title "Son of Man," we need to find the first time he used that title. It's in the story of the paralyzed man who was lowered down through the roof, into a house, in the midst of a large crowd of people. The story has a few surprises along the way: there was the urgency that must have been there in the mind of the man himself; and the boldness, or even audacity, of the four men who brought him and got him to the attention of Jesus. Then the words of Jesus were completely unexpected: "Son, your sins are forgiven." Some scribes are there, near enough to see and hear Jesus, and we can virtually hear what they're thinking: "Why does this man speak in this way? It is blasphemy! Who is able to forgive sins -- except only God?"

Jesus, aware of their thoughts, responded in a surprising way by tying together two things in the man's life: his severe disability, which everyone could see, and whatever sins he had, which might never be seen by anyone. Jesus confronted the scribes (who could neither forgive sins nor perform miracles of healing) and asked which was the easier. They had no answer.

Then Jesus gave a demonstration: "so that you can know that *the Son of Man* has authority on earth to forgive sins -- " and at this point Jesus turned to the paralytic and said, "-- get up, take up your mat, and go to your home."

Questioner: So in this brief narrative description about words and thoughts and surprises, Jesus made it brilliantly clear that when he said "Son of Man" he meant himself, for it was he who forgave the man's sins, and the forgiveness was demonstrated by the visible proof of the healing. Let me suggest how Peter and James might have described the event afterwards.

> "Man, have we had a busy time the past two weeks! And the crowds -- news about the teacher has been traveling like wildfire. When

we got back home here in Capernaum, I thought we might have a little time to rest up. By the way, how are things with your father by now, James?"

"Funny that you should ask. You remember how bent out of shape abba was when John and I dropped everything and just suddenly began following Jesus, leaving him and the staff, just the three of them to do the work that the five of us had been doing. He didn't get over it all the time we were traveling through Galilee. But he sincerely wanted to understand us, and Jesus too. So our abba was one of the first people there when he heard that Jesus was going to preach in the Mordecai house yesterday. You probably saw him there, Peter. He was in about the third row back."

"Yes, I did see him. Did he say anything about it later?"

"He sure did. He has a totally changed attitude. He told John and me to go on following Jesus, and to be as close to him as we could. He was especially moved by the whole episode of Reuben, the paralyzed man -- I guess everybody was, except those five scribes. The way the Teacher could tell exactly what they were thinking -- wow!"

"Yes, James, but even I could tell that they were not simpatico with the Teacher. But of course Jesus handled it all so easily! Without any sort of insult to them, Jesus pointed out that his abilities and his authority were altogether different from theirs."

> "Yes, and the way he connected together forgiveness and healing, it connected the visible change with the invisible, saying that if he couldn't do the invisible forgiveness, neither should Reuben be able to walk, either. But if he could walk then the forgiveness must be real, too. Our father Zebedee got the point very clearly. It was that that made Abba Zebedee change his mind about John and me becoming fishers of men."
>
> "Congratulations on that. But did you or John get what Jesus meant about the 'Son of Man'?"
>
> "Sure, Peter. Even our abba understood that. Jesus said "the Son of Man has authority on earth to forgive sins." Then *he* went ahead and forgave Reuben's sins as he healed him. So it was obvious that Jesus himself is willing to be known as the Son of Man. It means that he has authority directly from God. I just wonder if there is more to that title than we know."

So in Mark 2:10-11 it is clear that Jesus himself is the Son of Man, and that he claims *authority* from God to forgive sins, something totally unknown in Israel outside of him.

Questioner continues: In his timeless book *Mere Christianity,* C.S. Lewis examines the idea that many people hold, that we should just acknowledge Jesus as a moral teacher -- perhaps the greatest ever -- but that it is a step too far to accept him as God's Son. This is a tempting idea, and it has come up in every generation for nearly 300 years. Many people have settled for that view of Jesus.

However, drawing on this very passage in Mark 2, C.S. Lewis rules out the possibility. Here is his logic:

> 1. Jesus claimed to be the Son of God, and therefore not merely an ordinary man.
> 2. He also claimed to be able to forgive sins, something no ordinary man could do.
> 3. If he could not forgive sins and knew it, he was a liar.
> 4. If he was a liar, he was not a "moral teacher."
> 5. If he could not forgive sins but *believed* he could, he was crazy, a lunatic.
> 6. So, he was one of the three: Liar, Lunatic, or else he is Lord.

Here is part of the passage in *Mere Christianity* (page 56)

> I am trying here to prevent anyone saying the really foolish thing that people often say about Him: "I'm ready to accept Jesus as a great moral teacher, but I don't accept His claim to be God." That is the one thing we must not say. A man who was merely a man and said the sort of things Jesus said would not be a great moral teacher. He would either be a lunatic -- on a level with the man who says he is a poached egg -- or else he would be the Devil of Hell. You must make your choice. Either this man was, and is, the Son of God: or else a madman or something worse. You can shut Him up for a fool, you can spit at Him and kill Him as a demon; or you can fall at His feet and call Him Lord and God. But let us not come with any patronising

nonsense about his being a great human teacher. He has not left that open to us. He did not intend to.

This is a clear explanation, from that most reasonable and logical Christian thinker. Lewis does not mention it, but in this passage that is so full of surprises the title "Son of Man" is a key point. "...But so that you will know that the Son of Man has authority on earth to forgive sins ..."

Mark: There is one more very important point to focus on. Early in the Old Testament, before the people of Israel had entered the Promised Land, the question came up about true and false prophets: "How can we determine who is a true spokesman for God?"

> *Deuteronomy 18:14-22 ...These nations, which you are about to dispossess, listen to fortune-tellers and to diviners. But as for you, the LORD your God has not allowed you to do this. 15 "The LORD your God will raise up for you a prophet like me from among you, from your brothers—it is to him you shall listen— 16 just as you desired of the LORD your God at Horeb on the day of the assembly, when you said, 'Let me not hear again the voice of the LORD my God or see this great fire any more, lest I die.'*
>
> *17 And the LORD said to me, 'They are right in what they have spoken. 18 I will raise up for them a prophet like*

> *you from among their brothers. And I will put my words in his mouth, and he shall speak to them all that I command him. 19 And whoever will not listen to my words that he shall speak in my name, I myself will require it of him. 20 But the prophet who presumes to speak a word in my name that I have not commanded him to speak, or who speaks in the name of other gods, that same prophet shall die.'*
>
> *21 And if you say in your heart, 'How may we know the word that the LORD has not spoken?' 22 -- when a prophet speaks in the name of the LORD, <u>if the word does not come to pass or come true</u>, that is a word that the LORD has not spoken; the prophet has spoken it presumptuously. You need not be afraid of him.*

In this passage from the Torah, which we could think of as *'the law of the prophet,'* Deuteronomy 18:21-22 is the crucial part. If someone claims to be a prophet there should be a demonstration that the authority of God stands behind the person's message. "...if the word does not come to pass or come true ..." This implies that there should be an element of *prediction* in or alongside of the message that claims to be from God. Most often in the life of our people Israel this took the form of *"a sign."* There are specific references to signs in biblical passages such as Isaiah 7:14 ("the Lord himself will give you a sign"),

Exodus 4:8-9 (the signs of Moses' staff and leprous hand), or as Gideon said to the angel, "If now I have found favor in your eyes, then show me a sign that it is you who speaks to me" (Judges 6:17).

Often signs are given without being named as signs (see 2 Kings 2:6-14). In keeping with this pattern in the older Scriptures it is natural to consider Jesus' word about forgiveness and the healing of the paralyzed man as the word of God accompanied by a sign.

Questioner: Thank you, Mark. With these Old Testament passages in mind, I think I understand how *son of man* can also signify a person who is given a message with the authority of God Himself. And clearly Jesus had that purpose, that authority.

Later in the same chapter, that is, your second chapter, Jesus was challenged by the Pharisees for a simple act that his disciples were doing on the Sabbath -- merely plucking heads of ripe grain to eat on the spot. Jesus answered with a question: it was about King David even before he was king, bending a worship rule a thousand years earlier for the sake of hunger, and then Jesus led the discussion back to the Sabbath with two authoritative pronouncements:

Here is another "Son of Man" saying, and this one, too, presents him as speaking with spiritual authority.

> And he said to them, *"The Sabbath was made for man, not man for the Sabbath.* (2:27)
>
> *So the Son of Man is lord even of the Sabbath."* (2:28)

In the life of Israel the Sabbath stood out as the highest and holiest of the gifts of God, equaled only by the Temple.

Many rabbis and teachers in Israel may have had disciples. John the Baptist had disciples (see Matthew 11:2-4 and Mark 2:18), and so did the Pharisees. The disciples of any teacher were under the direction of their teacher. They were responsible *to* the teacher, and the teacher was responsible *for* them. Who did Jesus think he was, to allow his disciples to perform this act, plucking heads of wheat or barley, against the tradition of the scribes, on the Sabbath? Not only that, but when the Pharisees called explicit attention to this action, he justified their behavior, claiming to be the *son of man,* and *lord* over what can be permitted on the Sabbath.

When he said this, he claimed to be the one person who had authority higher than theirs: higher than the high priest, higher than the entire ruling council, the Sanhedrin. It was a bold claim, the kind of claim no one else could make: he could forgive sins and demonstrate by a powerful sign that he had the authority from God; and he could go over their heads and define or even re-define the Sabbath law.

How could these leaders accept a teacher like that? His actions, his words, his whole attitude was far outside the boundaries of acceptable tolerance. It's no wonder that he became the object of their disapproval.

On the other hand, the ordinary people had no such problem. It was for exactly that reason that they welcomed him.

"And they were astonished at his teaching, for he taught them as one who had authority, and not as the scribes." (1:22)

"And they were all amazed, so that they questioned among themselves, saying, 'What is this? A new teaching with authority!' (1:27)

Where we are so far:

Mark: You asked for an explanation of the times Jesus called himself Son of Man. I think I've answered your question about Jesus' use of the term, beginning with the fact that he meant himself, not some other person. Now I'm showing you the *three different kinds* of Son of Man references that Jesus made. The first two are:

1. The Son of Man who is persecuted and ultimately killed
2. The Son of Man who is Authoritative (and able to speak for God).

All three kinds of Son of Man sayings are dramatic and bold, but the third is the boldest of them all.

The Son of Man: Coming in the Clouds at the End of Time

On three separate occasions Jesus spoke of himself as the Son of Man with reference to the *future end of time.*

Jesus had called together his disciples together with "the crowd" (or multitude) and gave them instructions about what, for the follower of Christ, must be the important things in life. He begins,

> **If anyone wishes to follow after me, he must deny himself and take up his cross and follow.** (8:34)
>
> **For whoever wishes to save his life will lose it, and whoever loses his life for my sake and the sake of the Gospel, will save it.** (8:35)

This crowd included some people who were already disciples of Jesus and others who weren't. Even at this stage, pretty late in his ministry Jesus is inviting new disciples to join him. The group of the Twelve is complete and won't be enlarged, of course, but for serious followers (disciples in the larger sense of the word, as Jesus sometimes used it) there is always the invitation. That's still true. And the invitation then, as now, carries with it the most serious of challenges.

We shouldn't underestimate how serious this challenge is. To "deny" yourself doesn't merely mean to withhold from yourself some little indulgence or luxury (or even a big one). And what Jesus is talking about is not just something added to the old way of life. Jesus insisted that it's letting the old go, and accepting a change of personality and character from the normal life, to a totally different commitment.

This isn't even "reinventing" yourself: it means a willingness to let *Christ* reinvent you.

Questioner: So then, Mark, I would say that this is a pretty dynamic introduction to what it means to be a follower or disciple of Christ. But I don't see any clear reference to the *son of man* in the verses you quoted. Are we off the track a little?

Mark: No, we aren't off-track at all; but we need to go on for a few verses to make it clear. Speaking of a challenge from Jesus, here is the rest of it, following immediately after the words that I just quoted:

You can see that without a pause Jesus went further, bringing to our minds a very brief description of divine judgment at the end of time.

For what shall it profit a person to gain the whole world, and in the bargain lose his or her soul? For what can a person give to buy the soul back?

For whoever is ashamed of me and of my words in this adulterous and sinful generation, the Son of Man will be ashamed when he comes in the glory of his father with the holy angels. (8:36-38)

Can this be the same Son of Man, the same person, that Jesus has been speaking about? There is the Son of Man who makes a claim to forgive sins and to be lord of the Sabbath, and the Son of Man who will suffer greatly, and even die, at the hands of men? And now he will come in the glory of his Father with the holy angels?

This is not the only quotation of the kind. A very short time before the persecutions actually took place -- the physical, brutal ones -- Jesus spoke in detail about signs of the end of time. While he was impressing on the disciples the vision of that time to come he spoke about himself, again with the title *the Son of Man.*

> But be on guard; I have told you all things beforehand. But in those days, after that tribulation, the sun will be darkened, and the moon will not give its light, and the stars will be falling from heaven, and the powers in the

heavens will be shaken. And *then they will see the Son of Man* coming in clouds with great power and glory. And then he will send out the angels and gather his elect from the four winds, from the ends of the earth to the ends of heaven. (13:23-27)

Here in the midst of the final week of Jesus' life Jesus included a lengthy teaching on the end times. One of the disciples called attention to the massive stones that were part of Herod's enlargement and restoration work on the Temple. There were many local synagogues, wherever there were Israelites; but there was only one Temple. Herod had taken on the great task of enlargement and restoration of the Temple -- with hewn stones as large as four feet high, and four feet wide, and some nearly forty feet long, and weighing up to 140,000 pounds (70 tons). When one of the disciples comments on the wonderful stones, Jesus redirects the attention of them all away from the timeless stones of the Temple to the time when the Temple would be destroyed entirely. Then four of the disciples asked him directly about the signs of the time of fulfillment.

Mark continues: Their question was more about the time of the destruction of the Temple than about the time of the end. In his long answer Jesus wove together truth about (1) the time of terrible tribulation that was to come upon Jerusalem, and (2) the time of the end, after "nation will rise against nation, and kingdom against kingdom, ...earthquakes in various places, ...famines.... But the one who endures to the end will be saved." (Mark 13:8-13)

The time of the end that Jesus included is a time of the greatest tribulation in the world's history (verse 19) -- and after that tribulation "the sun will be darkened, and the moon will not give its light, and the stars will be falling from heaven, ...and *then they will see the Son of Man* coming in clouds with great power and glory" (verses 24-26). So this vision of the end of time is at the same time a vision of the Son of Man.

How can the Son of Man be the one who suffers and dies, and also the one who speaks with the authority of God, and also the one who appears to great throngs of people when the sun is darkened, the moon does not give its light and the stars are falling from heaven -- how can the same person take up all three of these differing roles? One more verse, and I will make it clear.

The verse I have in mind is Jesus' answer to the challenge of the high priest, at a hearing or trial before the Jewish ruling council: "are you the Christ, the Son of the Blessed?" Jesus' reply was direct and simple, but not subtle: "I am," and in those two words alone he laid claim to two high titles, *Christ* and *Son of God*. But he adds, "... and you will see *the Son of Man*_seated at the right hand of Power and *coming with the clouds of heaven*."

Questioner: Wow, Mark, That's a lot of information to think about. Can you go over it, or maybe summarize, so I can be sure I'm getting your point?

Mark: Sure -- I'll be glad to do that. But there is a third very important truth in Jesus' answer, and so as part of my summary and explanation I think I should give you *Two Specialized Words.* You probably know I stayed away from long words and technical phrases in my writing. I know that words can sometimes get in the way of clear understanding -- but here is a case where longer words can help us to be clear.

Eschatology: This is a word that describes God's control of the future, and includes the end times.

Apocalyptic: This is a word that describes the destruction of the world, or at least drastic changes in all the things we are used to. This kind of teaching uses extravagant, compelling images such as "the sun will be darkened," "stars will fall", and so forth.

Apocalyptic thought is always eschatological, but many things that are eschatological are not apocalyptic. Both of these words describe future times. *Eschatology* describes "whatever God has planned for any time in the future." That could indicate God's action within human history, such as new leadership for God's covenant-people, or even a new leader for another nation.

But *apocalyptic* ideas are different. They tell us of a coming upheaval and destruction at the end of the world as we know it. Most often, however, the apocalyptic teaching includes God's action in rebuilding: *new heavens and new earth; final judgment; new Jerusalem; no night there* -- these are all part of the apocalyptic teachings you can find in the Bible.

At his trial, the high priest asked Jesus to "incriminate" himself with the claim to be the Christ, and the Son of "the Blessed" (that is, the Son of God). He answered, "I am; and you will see the son of man seated at the right hand of Power and coming with the clouds of heaven." No doubt this is not the answer the high priest expected, but it was a three-part claim by Jesus. Son of God, Son of Man, and the apocalyptic man who is timeless and at God's right hand.

Son of Man in the Old Testament

The Son of Man was Important in the Old Testament, the Scriptures that Jesus knew

Questioner: None of the New Testament was written down until years after the death of Christ; but Jesus knew the Old Testament very well. He quoted it often during the years of his mission, and this continued even while he was dying on the cross.

Mark: There are three important kinds of use of the phrase "the son of man" in the Scriptures that Jesus knew and used. Each one of these is very important for you to understand.

1. Son of man in Psalms

In the Book of Psalms (which is almost totally poetic, in the Hebrew style of poetry) the term "son of man" is used poetically as a synonym of "human." The term is used in the same way in at least twelve locations in the Old Testament. They are all interesting, and one of them very picturesque (Job 25:4-6, in a speech by Bildad the Shuhite).

> *How then can a man be righteous*
>   *before God?*
> *How can one born of woman be pure?*
> *If even the moon is not bright,*
> *and the stars are not pure in his eyes,*
> *how much less man, who is but a maggot --*
> ***a son of man****, who is only a worm*!

Here I'll quote just three references in the Book of Psalms.

> *When I look at your heavens,*
> *the work of your fingers, the moon and the stars which you have set in place,*
> *what is **man** that you are mindful of him, and the **son of man** that you care for him?"* (Psalm 8:4)

Here the meaning of *man* and *son of man* is the same. Hebrew poetry often had two parallel lines, both meaning the same thing, expressed in different words for clearer understanding. Here is an example of that parallel style from Proverbs 19:6:

> Many seek the favor of a generous man;
> and everyone is a friend to a man who gives gifts.

"A generous man" is parallel in meaning to "a man who gives gifts," and "many seek the favor of" is the same as "everyone is a friend of."

Now here is another "son of man" reference from the Book of Psalms.

*"O LORD, what is man that you regard him, or the **son of man** that you think of him?"* (Psalm 144:3) This is identical in meaning to Psalm 8:4 above.

Here is a third:

*"Put not your trust in princes, in **a son of man**, in whom there is no salvation."* Psalm 146:3   Here the meaning of the passage is, Do not put your trust in princes, because they are only human and are powerless to grant salvation.

You can see that one of the ways "son of man" is used is sometimes as a synonym for "person," without further explanation.

2: " Son of man" in Ezekiel

The prophet Ezekiel lived in the time of the Babylonian exile, when large numbers of the people of Judea were taken as captives to Babylon, about 50 miles from modern Baghdad (and nearly 600 miles from Jerusalem). Ezekiel was among them, and he received a series of visions and messages from the Lord for the Jewish people who were in Babylon.

The book of the prophet Ezekiel uses the term *"son of man"* often -- more often than all the rest of the Bible combined, 93 times in all. Ezekiel's usage is not like the Book of Psalms, meaning "human."

- It is always a term referring to Ezekiel himself.

- Every single time the term appears, it is God speaking directly to Ezekiel.
- It always is a term that alerts us, as readers of Ezekiel's message, to the fact that this is important. Like saying "listen up!"
- Nearly every time it is God showing Ezekiel something or giving him a message to pass on to the people. "Tell them this for me."

As I said, ninety-three examples can be found. Here are just a few of them.

"And he said to me, "**Son of man**, go to the house of Israel and speak with my words to them." (Ezekiel 3:4)

"So you, **son of man**, I have made a watchman for the house of Israel. Whenever you hear a word from my mouth, you shall give them warning from me." (Ezekiel 33:7)

"**Son of man**, how does the wood of the vine surpass any wood, the vine branch that is among the trees of the forest? (Ezekiel 15:2)

"**Son of man**, make known to Jerusalem her abominations (Ezekiel 16:2)

"**Son of man**, propound a riddle, and speak a parable to the house of Israel (Ezekiel 17:2)

"**Son of man**, speak to the elders of Israel, and say to them, Thus says the

> Lord God, Is it to inquire of me that you come? As I live, declares the Lord God, I will not be inquired of by you.
> (Ezekiel 20:3)

Over and over Ezekiel receives messages or visions, and with them he also gets specific instructions on how to deliver them.

So this part of the Old Testament is full of the term *son of man*, and is used to designate the prophet <u>when he is speaking for God</u>. You may be able to see how this was applicable to Jesus, too. There are places in my Gospel account where Jesus spoke with the authority of God. In chapter 2, for example, look at verses 5, 10-11, and 27-28.

Questioner: Mark, can I interrupt you for a minute? What you've said so far is true, and it's well-said. And maybe you're getting to it, but what you've said so far doesn't quite put it together. There has to be something more.

I remember a man I met several years ago in Oxford, England, who spent much of his life trying to prove that the New Testament was wrong about Jesus. He had even written books that sought to present that case.

The thing he was trying to prove was that Jesus was just one of a number of traveling teachers that gathered disciples and traveled around Judea and Galilee teaching about God and the world, about right and wrong. Nothing very special about Jesus. He was just typical. This scholar's theory was that when Jesus' followers *wrote* about him they began to exaggerate and claim that he could perform miracles of healing, multiplying loaves and fishes, even walk on the water.

This man seemed convinced that these things couldn't be true of Jesus. They couldn't be true of any man. So for him Jesus was an ordinary man, an excellent teacher, but nothing more.

In a long time of conversation the same man said this to me, and it was a bombshell: "I have no problem accepting that Jesus called himself 'son of God.' We're all sons of God. You are. I am. But what I can't accept is that he ever called himself *son of man*."

He said it as though acceptance that Jesus used that term would destroy this scholar's whole life's work.

I didn't ask any questions, but I wondered, *"what is there in the title Son of Man that this scholar can't accept? There must be more to it than I understand."* So in the next few weeks I went to the Old Testament and studied up on it. I think I've got it now, but I'd like to have you go on, to make it very clear for my readers.

Mark: I'll be glad to, but you (and your readers) need to keep in mind that all three of these are important, and this third one is the most important of them all.

3. The Apocalyptic Son of Man in Daniel

Back to my written account of Jesus for a minute: you recall that when Jesus spoke to the disciples about the end times he said, "And then they will see the Son of Man coming in clouds with great power and glory." (That's in Mark 13:26.) When Jesus says something, I believe him, that isn't in question. But when he tied the *Son of Man* with "coming in clouds with great power and glory," Jesus was referring to one specific part of the Old Testament.

The Book of Daniel, the next book after Ezekiel, has in it several apocalyptic visions. The vision in chapter 7 is a stirring portrayal of great kingdoms and world empires, all of them having tremendous power, but also marked by ruthless use of that power. We can try to identify these as the Assyrian, the Babylonian, the Persian, and the Greek empires, all appearing in only eight verses. Then when the final empire loses its power, the scene changes. "As I looked, thrones were placed, and the Ancient of Days took his seat...." Then there is a brief description of the Ancient of Days, the vision's representation of God -- with even a brief description of his throne: "His throne was fiery flames; its wheels were burning fire."

> A stream of fire issued and came out from before him; a thousand thousands served him, and ten thousand times ten thousand stood before him; the court sat in judgment, and the books were opened. [*This looks like the scene of the final judgment, with millions*

> *and millions of the people of earth standing before God, the Judge.*]
>
> "I looked then because of the sound of the great words that the horn was speaking [*this is a horn on the fourth beast-empire*]. And as I looked, the beast was killed, and its body destroyed and given over to be burned with fire.
>
> As for the rest of the beasts, their dominion was taken away, but their lives were prolonged for a season and a time.
>
> "I saw in the night visions, and behold, with the clouds of heaven there came <u>one like a son of man</u>, and he came to the Ancient of Days and was presented before him.
>
> And to him was given dominion and glory and a kingdom, that all peoples, nations, and languages should serve him; his dominion is an everlasting dominion, which shall not pass away, and his kingdom one that shall not be destroyed.   (-- Daniel 7:10-14)

When it says "one like a son of man" the first meaning we considered is that this is one with the appearance of a human being, and that isn't so far from the meaning of "son of man" in Psalm 8:4, Psalm 144:3, and Psalm 146:3. In those places it means "strictly human." But in Daniel 7:13 the *son of man* is not so limited -- in fact he is not limited at all. Here is a simple analysis of the verses in Daniel 7:

- Millions of people are gathered before the presence of The Ancient of Days (God).

- The Court sat in judgment (verse 10)
- The Books were opened -- for (the final) judgment. (verse 10)
- With the clouds of heaven there came one like a "son of man." (verse 13)
- The "son of man" was presented before the Ancient of Days. (verse 13)
- To the Son of Man was given **dominion, glory, and a kingdom**.
- All peoples, nations, and languages (that is, all the people of the world) will honor and serve the Son of Man (verse 14)
- The kingdom and rule of the Son of Man will last forever, in contrast to the great empires of the world, which earlier parts of chapter 7 dramatically portray. (verses 2 through 8, 11-12, and then verse 14)
- The Son of Man at the end of time will be given everlasting dominion.

Now back to Son of Man in the Gospel of Mark

Mark continues: Three separate times Jesus made the claim that he was the Son of Man in words that link himself with the Son of Man in that great passage in Daniel 7.

At his trial, a trial that was not legitimate even by their own rules, false witnesses were secured by "the chief priests and the whole council." Even then, they could not find two false witnesses that agreed. So Jesus was interrogated by the high priest, the one man who was presiding elder over the priests of Israel.

For a while, Jesus remained silent; but then a second round of questioning began -- with a most direct question. "Are you the Christ, the son of the Blessed?" This question Jesus answered directly, with a two-part answer: **"I am; and you will see the Son of Man seated at the right-hand side of power, and coming with the clouds of heaven."**

Jesus was on trial for his life. Yet this answer of Jesus in Mark 14:62 was bold and forceful. It was a message with *apocalyptic* flavor -- remember, apocalyptic is teaching about the end of the world, upheaval and upsetting almost everything we know of nature (how else could he come *with the clouds of heaven*?), and a final judgment. There, in front of the religious ruling council, the claim that he put forth was a challenge including four separate things they could not accept. In answering the high priest he claimed to be--

- the Christ, the Messiah who was to come with God's message and power,

- the Son of the Blessed. That was the high priest's way of saying Son of God. Jewish people usually avoided using the name of

God whenever possible to avoid possibilities of taking His name in vain,

- the Son of Man, in particular the Son of Man as in Daniel 7, who receives glory, everlasting dominion, a kingdom that will not be destroyed, that all peoples of all nations and languages should serve him.

- the one who is seated at God's right hand and coming in the clouds of heaven.

The leaders of Israel, whether priests or scribes, Pharisees or Sadducees, had concluded that Jesus was to be rejected. Now his answer to the high priest also had to be rejected as well, immediately and categorically.

Questioner: I need to interrupt again for a minute -- but this is the very reason my unbelieving friend said he *couldn't* accept that Jesus called himself "son of man." This friend was trying to pick and choose the parts of the accounts like yours about Jesus, Mark -- with no more reason for the need to accept and reject than merely his own personal preferences. It's obvious that he wasn't basing his preferences on thoughtful logic or evidence, but on his preconceived notion. It's as if he was saying, "Of course Jesus couldn't have used the title 'son of man,' because that would make my whole theory wrong -- and my theory isn't wrong!"

But he taught me something I hadn't yet discovered. His statement made me go back to the

Bible and take another, more careful look at **Son of Man** in Mark, and see if I hadn't been missing something important. And sure enough, I had. Now back to you, Mark. Thanks for letting me break in here.

Mark: No problem at all. At this point I can briefly sum up. In my account of the Gospel I've included two other times Jesus tied his title *son of man* to the times of the end. He taught on the frightful future for Jerusalem.

> And Jesus said to him, "Do you see these great buildings? There will not be left here one stone upon another that will not be thrown down." (13:2
>
> But be on your guard. For they will deliver you over to councils, and you will be beaten in synagogues, and you will stand before governors and kings for my sake, to bear witness before them. (13:9)

-- And the tribulations at the end times for the world

> For in those days there will be such tribulation as has not been from the beginning of the creation that God created until now, and never will be. And if the Lord had not cut short the days, no human being would be saved. But for the sake of the elect, whom he chose, he shortened the days. (13:19 - 20)

He taught these things all in one day during the week before his death, and he wove those two subjects together, with the meaning included that God is in the future for all those who depend on him. In that 13th chapter Christ also includes these words: "*And then they will see the <u>Son of Man coming in clouds with great power and glory</u>.*" (Mark 13:26)

Of course it's easy to see that he's talking about the time of the ultimate judgment.

Even earlier he had issued a warning to the multitude of his hearers, including his disciples.
"For whoever is ashamed of me and my words in this immoral and sin-filled generation, of him will <u>the Son of Man </u>also be ashamed, <u>when he comes in the glory of his Father with the holy angels</u>. (8:38)

Chapter 12

The Key Verse in Mark

MARK 10:45

Questioner: Mark, I paused to count the number of times "Son of Man" appears in your Gospel account. There are thirteen of them, nearly enough to have one in each chapter. In our conversations you have actually made reference to almost all of them. You're right, too: all those you've mentioned fit neatly into those three categories, **(1)** *The man who is human, and vulnerable to being persecuted and dying, though he will rise again;* **(2)** *The man whom God grants authority to speak for Him;* and **(3)** *The one who is far beyond human, who will come with clouds and will have all authority and dominion at the end of the world's time.* In brief terms they can be called

1. Suffering,
2. Authoritative,
3. Apocalyptic.

But, Mark, when I counted the ones you commented on, I believe you have come up just a bit short. There are 13 passages, but you have commented on only twelve. Have you forgotten one?

Mark: Ah, yes -- but there's no mistake, I'm coming to that one. You're right that there is one that I haven't mentioned. It's in chapter ten. I wanted to call attention to that saying of Jesus separately because it is so important. Some people even think of it as "*the key verse*" of my Gospel account, in the sense that it gives perspective to many other things that Jesus taught. Here it is, the one verse I omitted in my discussion just now. I'm interested in hearing your comments on it.

> *For even the Son of Man did not come to be served but to serve, and to give his life as a ransom for many.*
> (Mark 10:45)

Questioner: Mark, you've really put me on the spot, asking me -- without warning -- to comment on a major verse like this one. This verse does really put together the entire purpose of Jesus' life and ministry, doesn't it? I'm going to try to answer your question, and I need to treat it with as much seriousness as you have for the questions I've asked you. I'm going to try to do that in three parts.

1. Jesus has just challenged all followers of whatever level, to take the position of the servant. Then he intentionally includes himself as the benchmark for the Servant Challenge. To follow him is just that: to follow, and to take the position of a servant just as Jesus did.

2. This verse serves to interpret for us both the *motivation* and the *goal* in the life of Jesus. It reminds us just how purposed and intentional he was. Giving his life was neither incidental nor accidental. His death on the cross cannot be understood apart from the goal, and it is a goal that he willingly accepted. The *ransom* idea

means to pay a price for something that is not at the moment in your possession.

If you, or someone you love, is kidnapped and held for ransom you might pay a very high price -- higher than you can afford -- to set them free. The phrase "a king's ransom" is occasionally heard, and means a price higher than *any* ordinary person can afford. As a crime, kidnapping is rare in the United States, and in most countries with effective law enforcement. In countries where there is a strong element of lawlessness (such as drug cartels that are immune from prosecution because of their ruthless use of power) kidnapping is much more common.

Questioner continues: In the history of Israel, under some circumstances a person who deserved the death penalty could have his or her life redeemed by paying a ransom: "he shall give for the redemption of his life whatever is imposed on him." (Exodus 21:30) In some passages we are reminded that a slave could be ransomed and set free.

But though the psalmist makes it emphatic that human life cannot be extended through paying a ransom to God, for the price would be higher than anyone could pay. (Psalm 49:7-8) All alike, whether rich or poor, will die. Yet just a bit further along in the same psalm comes the affirmation, "But God will ransom my soul from the power of the grave. He will receive me." (Psalm 49:15)

In the case of the verse 10:45, Jesus' claim is not made lightly. he has obviously thought carefully about the meaning, and declares himself, his life, in fact, to be "a ransom for many."

3. He also incorporates the deepest, most profound truth about the Son of Man: if he was the timeless, cosmic, powerful, apocalyptic Son of Man (and of course he was) then it is the greatest transformation of will we can imagine, for him to sacrifice his very life. The concept of ransom appears often in the ancient world, including the Old Testament, speaking of the ransom of Israel from bondage in Egypt. This thought is found, for example, in Isaiah 51:11:

> And the *ransomed* of the LORD shall return and come to Zion with singing; everlasting joy shall be upon their heads; they shall obtain gladness and joy, and sorrow and sighing shall flee away.

This verse looks not only to the past but also strongly to the future, looking forward to God's coming ransom of his people. Psalm 49:7 reflects on the truth that we all know, that all humans are destined to die, and that no one can become a ransom for another to change that fact.

> Truly no man can ransom another, or give to God the price of his life, for the ransom of their life is costly and can never suffice, that he should live on forever and never see the pit. Psalm 49:7-9

Christ, the Son of Man, was the one and only exception to this fact, prefigured in the same Psalm: "*But God will ransom my life from the grave; He will surely take me to himself.*" He alone can give his life as a ransom, and not merely for one person.

The most important fact and focus of the word *ransom* is in the Covenant. The people of Israel were the Covenant People of God, and the covenant with

Abraham at the beginning was brought into effect through the sacrifice of an animal. This was an act of ransom, or redemption, of the person or a group, or of the entire nation.

Through the many generations of the life of Israel there were times of covenant renewal, and always there was sacrifice. With careful thought and deep meaning, Jesus, one time for all (and I can also say once for all time), takes the place of the sacrifices of the Covenant.

> **...but to serve, and to give his life as a ransom for many.**

Mark: Thank you, Questioner. I think you've put a good conclusion on our discussion of Son of Man. I think we're ready now to go on to other questions, if you have them.

Questioner: Yes, Mark, I do have more questions. In fact, I have several more. For now, could we turn to the subject of miracles?

Chapter 13
Miracles

The Questioner continues: I'm familiar enough with your Gospel account to know that miracles are pretty important to your description of Jesus; and I'm sure that they were central to his own life and ministry, so I'd say that your emphasis is correct. One of the most striking features of your Gospel account, Mark, is the great number of miracles that you've included. You have listed about twenty separate miracles or miracle occasions. Even though yours is by far the shortest of the Gospels, you have nearly as many miracles as Matthew, who tells of 22, or Luke, who reports on 21 miracles.

Summaries of miracle occasions

Mark, in a couple of places you make summary statements about miracles, and without any specific description you gather together some occasion -- or in one place it is a larger *series* of occasions -- and give a summary of the healing activities of Jesus. We'll watch for them. The first one of these is in your first chapter, following right after your description of the first two miracles.

Man with an unclean spirit

Soon after Jesus began his public ministry, following his baptism at the hands of John the Baptist, he began to preach about the reign of God, repentance, and faith. He challenged the first four of his disciples to follow him, and while they were in Capernaum, when the Sabbath came he taught in the synagogue. There was a man in the synagogue with "an unclean spirit," and the spirit tried to engage Jesus in a dispute -- in fact the evil spirit carries on the dispute alone: "What business do you have with us? Have you come to destroy us? I know you, and I know who you are: the holy one of God!" (1:23-27)

Jesus demanded silence from the unclean spirit, and then he commanded the spirit to leave the man. The immediate result was obvious. The spirit left the man at Jesus' command. This caused amazement in all the people there, who exclaimed to one another how extraordinary that was; and in particular that he could command evil spirits and they obeyed him.

Peter's Mother-in-law

Immediately after this event in the synagogue, Jesus went to Simon's house with those four disciples that he had called: Simon, Andrew, James and John. Simon's mother-in-law was sick with a fever, but Jesus healed her in taking her by the hand and lifting her up. Right away she was made well, and demonstrated her restored health by serving them. This took place within a private home -- Simon's -- and so there were no observers outside the committed circle of Jesus and his followers. As a result there is little feeling of amazement in the passage -- though we may ourselves feel that kind of wonder as we read the account. (1:29-31)

Now, Mark, in just eleven verses you've shown us three events: a synagogue service, a demon cast out after its noisy protest, and a woman cured of a fever. Then, as if it were the most ordinary thing in the world, you tell of an event that took place that very evening.

> That evening at sundown they brought to him all who were sick or oppressed by demons. And the whole city was gathered together at the door. And he healed many who were sick with various diseases, and cast out many demons. And he would not permit the demons to speak, because they knew him.(Mark 1:32-34)

Mark, this event is very different from the others. You describe it well, so we can begin to visualize the scene as it happened there in Capernaum. Your account is very short, only 54 words in four sentences in English, and in the Greek only 46 words. This is not the same kind of description we have in the two miracle accounts that you've included just before it. Those were descriptions of individual miracles, while this is a very brief summary of a larger event.

So, Mark, this doesn't mean that the individuals who were helped that evening were less important, or the miraculous change Jesus brought to them was less significant -- or does it?

Mark: No, no, I wouldn't want you to get that impression. My own view is that Jesus lived the fullest kind of life, and everything he did was intentional, and every person he met was important to him because he was filled with compassion. Maybe this is brought out clearly on the occasion when a woman touched the fringe of his garment in faith, in hope that she might be healed. It happened for her just as she hoped and believed.

Jesus knew something significant had happened through someone's faith -- for he had felt power go out of him -- and he felt he needed to find out who it was who had called forth his power. After he got the whole story from the woman he pronounced words of both power and compassion. He could so easily have gone on his way without seeking her out, but as I said, for him there were no unimportant people, no unimportant occasions.

I don't want to leave the impression that the many who were sick or oppressed by demons were less important. But there were so very many people like that, and since I had already written about two specific incidents I wanted to give a brief summary of Jesus' healing and casting out demons during that evening. You've noticed, probably, that the summary includes exactly (and only) the kind of acts of Jesus that I have described previously: healing the body and casting out unclean spirits.

It's easy to tell when you see a summary. Look for the general, "collective" words in the description: in this three-verse summary you'll see *all, whole, many,* and *various.* Then there is this way of showing repeated action: *would,* or *would not.* Here is that summary again, with the "summarizing" words underlined. I think you'll see what I mean.

> That evening at sundown they brought to him <u>all</u> *who were sick or oppressed by demons.* And <u>the whole</u> *city was gathered together at the door. And he healed* <u>many</u> *who were sick with* <u>various</u> *diseases, and cast out* <u>many</u> *demons. And he* <u>would not</u> *permit the demons to speak, because they knew him.* (Mark 1:32-34)

You'll find other summaries, and they include other sorts of miraculous acts, but in my writing they will only appear if a description of that act has been given previously. Here is an example:

And when they got out of the boat, the people immediately recognized him and ran about *the whole region* and *began* to bring the sick people on their beds to *wherever* they heard he was. And *wherever* he came, *in villages, cities, or countryside,* they laid the sick in the marketplaces and *implored him that they might touch even the fringe of his garment.* And *as many as* touched it were made well. (6:54-56)

Again I emphasized the summarizing words and phrases, and also I included the fact that that people were made well upon touching the fringe of his garment. I felt free to include this detail because the example of the healing power was described, about a chapter earlier. It is one of my unwritten rules -- not one of the most important things, but just the way I write -- that I will never include in a summary, something I have not earlier given in an example -- but you probably already knew that.

Questioner: Yes, Mark, I had noticed how careful you are on some details, but still it's good that you pointed that out. It's an interesting thing to keep in mind, because I've noticed that Matthew's and Luke's accounts don't follow your unwritten rule, as we see by simply looking at Matthew 4:23-25, and Luke 4:44, 6:17-19. Still, it helps me to value your carefulness in handling the facts.

Mark: Thank you very much. But don't give me too much credit. Remember, in writing a Gospel account the writer *intends* to stay in the background.

Questioner: Oh, yes, that brings to mind a question I should have asked earlier, but now is a very good time, though I hope in just a few minutes to bring the interview back to the Miracles of Jesus. Mark, I have the advantage that you did not have. I have the entire body of earliest inspired Christian writings that we call the New Testament; and in most of those books the writer is identified by name. It happens that you have not let your name be known anywhere in your writing. It turns out that none of the other writers of the Gospels have revealed their names, either.

How does it happen that you --I mean the four of you who wrote accounts of the Gospel -- all wrote anonymously? Is it coincidence, or was there some plan in place that the others should follow your pattern and also not take credit for their writings?

Mark: Good question! In my case, I felt so compelled to present the events in Jesus' life as clearly as possible, with no embellishment by me, and with as little interpretation as possible. My goal was always to write the truth, and to write simply. I may have been the *writer*, but Jesus himself is in a real sense the *author* of this action. Maybe it would be helpful to think of a play or drama, enacted on a stage. Somebody wrote it. You may even know who wrote it. But does the playwright call attention to herself or himself? No, the action on the stage speaks for itself, or the dialogue of the actors develops the message.

For my part, I like to think of myself as the person out of sight who draws open the curtain. I wasn't even there for most of the events of Jesus' life, though I had plenty of information from Peter and others who had been close to Jesus; and besides that, I firmly believe I had guidance also from the Spirit of God as I wrote.

Questioner: I noticed that you said that you weren't there "for most of the events of Jesus' life." From the way you said that, should we guess that you were present for some part of the unfolding of these events?

Mark: Well, as you know, our family owned a pretty sizable house in Jerusalem (Acts 12:12), and my mother, as a follower of Christ's message, was always happy to be the hostess when other believers gathered. So many of them were from Galilee, they were glad to have a welcoming place when they were in Jerusalem. I was not old enough to be away from home, and so I lived there with my mother.

Many of my readers have put a few clues together like this: in 14:51-52 you will find a bare glimpse of a young man who was following Jesus up to the moment of his arrest in Gethsemane. The detail is mentioned that he was not dressed; he had nothing but a linen cloth wrapped around his body. Well, it's short, I may as well quote it. *And a young man followed him, with nothing but a linen cloth about his body. And they seized him, but he left the linen cloth and ran away naked.*

There are many who suppose that young man was me, and the story follows Jesus' Passover meal with his disciples, which they suggest could well have been observed in our own family's upper room. Their theory also places me as present at, though a latecomer to, the garden. These people suggest that the brief episode is a little like an artist who doesn't sign his artistic work, but puts his or her initials in the corner of the canvas.

Questioner: So Mark, I need to ask --

Mark: -- And now I've got you wondering -- was I that young man? You don't really expect me to answer that, do you? I won't confirm or deny the notion, but I want to leave it as a puzzle for you and my other readers to ponder.

Questioner: All right, we won't pursue that question any further. We'll leave it right there. For right now, maybe we can go back to the subject of the miracles of Jesus.

Mark, you've written much more about miracles than some of the other aspects of Jesus' ministry. I've heard some people who live in my own time go to great lengths to argue that Jesus didn't *really* perform miracles. The argument usually goes something like this:

> "I don't live in a world in which people walk on water; therefore, of course, Jesus didn't really walk on the water. So what was it that actually happened, that the Gospel writers

(and the early church) exaggerated [or *expanded*, or *distorted*] into a miracle?"

Mark: It seems interesting, if that is really their way of thinking, that these people you speak of start with themselves and their own observations as their definition of what is real and what is not, or what is even more odd, that they could make their own experience the test of what is possible. This seems to mean that they've made a new rule: they will never believe in anything that they haven't themselves seen.

Questioner: Well, I'm sure that they would add that it's more complex than that, but that statement represents the philosophy of "rationalism," which begins by ruling out any possibility of supernatural events. In other words, God can't act in the physical world. The quotation I've given above was written by a scholar of some repute. The point he was making at the time seemed to be that anyone who believed in miracles was naive and gullible.

Mark: Oh yes, the old trick: "I can win the debate if you will agree to limit the evidence to what I say." If in advance you rule out the possibility that God can act in the world, then you rule out even the existence of God, and you rule out much on almost every page of my writing -- maybe on nearly every page of the Bible. At the same time you rule out the purpose of prayer, and heaven.

Naturally, this starts when a person decides to be the judge of what God can and cannot do. I've found it best to let God decide that for himself. The strong impression I get from every part of our Scriptures is that when people approach God with faith, they can see him at work. By the way, this draws us right back to the miracles of Jesus.

When Jesus went back to Nazareth, his home town (you can find that in 6:1-6), even in the face of evidence -- in his teaching, preaching, and in the reputation that had made him virtually famous through all Galilee -- he was met with skepticism. The townspeople recited the names of the members of his family and his experience as a carpenter, as though his roots, relationships, and routine occupation would shut out any possibility that he could have greater wisdom or power than the normal person. They did not believe: as a result, his power was limited.

God is always powerful; and Jesus as Son of God had authority, access to that power. Yet God is pleased to unleash his power when it meets with faith, and Jesus watched for faith in people he met. When four men were bringing the paralyzed man to Jesus for healing they were unable to bring him into Jesus' presence because of the great number of people and the small size of the house he was in. You remember that they went to the extreme measure of removing the tiles of the roof and let his pallet down right in front of Jesus. "And when Jesus saw *their* faith, he spoke to the paralyzed man ..." So Jesus took note of the faith that was there not only in the paralytic but in the friends who took such action.

There was a strange lack of faith expressed by the people of his home town, and as a result his power was limited. He was somehow prevented from doing any mighty works -- though as I wrote, he was able to heal a few sick people.

Questioner: What must that have been like for Jesus, to have a limitation on his ministry of healing directly because of unbelief?

Mark: Well, as you probably noticed I don't get into the feelings that Jesus had or his emotions, very much. I did focus on his anger a time or two. Anger, or indignation, must have been in his mind when he forcefully drove out from the temple "those who sold and those who bought in the temple, and overturned the tables of the money-changers... and he would not permit anyone to carry anything through the temple."

Also, there is the deep distress and great heaviness he experienced in Gethsemane. (14:32-34) And at a much earlier time, when the religious leadership was more concerned with what actions to avoid on the Sabbath than with the great need of a man who was severely disabled, he confronted them and asked, "Is it lawful on the Sabbath to do good, or to do harm? --To save life or to kill?" At that point Jesus scanned their faces and saw from that how hard their hearts were, "and he looked around at them with anger." (3:4-5) His anger at that time turned into a painful grief, or as I wrote, he was "grieved at their hardness of heart."

Jesus was the Son of God, and he was at the same time fully human. So in answer to your question, of course he was greatly disappointed at the rejection by his townspeople in Nazareth. I was thinking of his dismay when I wrote that he "marveled" at their unbelief . (6:1-6)

Questioner: In reading the accounts of some of the miracles, it is easy to see the compassion that Jesus had for people in distress.

Miracles and Jesus' Compassion

Clearly he was moved with compassion when he saw people who were suffering, or people who were at the point of losing hope. But there were other reasons, and other dynamics present when Jesus performed miracles, weren't there?

Mark: Yes, certainly. When the woman touched the fringe of his garment, Jesus wasn't aware of her need, or from Peter's account, even of her presence yet she was healed through her approach, her touch, and her faith. It is good to see, though, that Jesus gave confirmation *in words* of the healing that had taken place: "Daughter, your faith has saved you; go in peace and be wholly free from that which has plagued you." Even though it was not a part of the action of healing, certainly his compassion was present. This miracle, however, occurred purely because the power of the Father was so present in him, when met by her faith.

Miracles as Signs

As you know, I was brought up in an observant Jewish home. My schooling and my city were also traditional and Jewish as well. In such an environment it was always well understood that any spokesperson for the Lord must have a means of demonstrating his authenticity. Usually this took the form of a *sign*, as we see in Isaiah 7:14 ("therefore the Lord himself will give you a sign..."). This is in accord with Deuteronomy 18:21-22. You'll recall that I've mentioned it before, but let me refer to it once more.

> And if you say in your heart, 'How may we know the word that the LORD has not spoken?' — when a prophet speaks in the name of the LORD, if the word does not come to pass or come true, that is a word that the LORD has not spoken; the prophet has spoken it presumptuously. You need not be afraid of him.

"*If the word does not come to pass or come true*" shows the need for an element of prediction in the words of anyone who claims to speak for God. This was a sign -- it would always be of an unexpected nature, often a miracle.

Questioner: All of Jesus' public miracles could have been interpreted even by those who opposed him, as signs. Yet more than once the opponents requested a sign from him, in the face of signs all around them, wherever Jesus went. As a result Jesus made no secret of his impatience with their request. "No sign," he said. Matthew and Luke later gave the fuller quotation, "No sign but that of Jonah."

Mark: But of course Jesus tailored his answers to the minds, and sincerity, of the people asking. So there was a time when John the Baptist sent a question for Jesus from prison, "Are you the one?" In answer, Jesus sent the baptist's disciples back with a mental list of the signs they had seen. In the Book of Isaiah each of these things is tied in as a mark or characteristic of the age of fulfillment, the times of the Messiah. Calling attention to the miraculous works of Jesus, naturally, should be all the answer John would need.

Miracles Demonstrate Jesus' Power

If we're counting, let's look at another reason for Jesus' miracle work; and let's call it reason number three. Numbers one and two were:

1. The **compassion** Jesus had for people in need.

2. Miracles served as **signs** that Jesus spoke the truth and spoke for God.

Now here is reason number three:

3. Miracles are a **demonstration of the power that was in Jesus**.

You can see in accounts of the life of Jesus, that time after time when he performed a miraculous act people were amazed, they marveled, they were astonished, they were utterly astounded, or they were filled with wonder. And the reason is that in his miracles the power that was in Jesus Christ came to the forefront and was displayed for others to see. Normally this power was not visible to the eyes, in the same way that his identity or nature as God was not seen -- except on the rarest of occasions, such as the transfiguration. To most people Jesus looked so ordinary, and even those closest to him may have needed an extraordinary event from time to time to perceive better who he was, or to reinforce what they were beginning to understand about him.

As examples of the reaction of people to the wonders Jesus accomplished, I'll just name two: when Jesus healed the paralytic (and forgave the man's sins) the spirit, or attitude, of amazement came over them, but all they could say was, "we've never seen anything like this." (2:12) Quite a while later, after several notable healing miracles the people who were there "were astonished beyond measure," and they said, "He has done all things well. He even causes the deaf to hear and the mute to speak." (7:37)

Questioner: Yes, Mark, I can see that. Often people were amazed at the works of Jesus; and also by his teachings, as I read in your Gospel account.

But surely Jesus didn't perform miracles, thus in some measure changing the dynamics of heaven and earth, just to amaze the multitudes, did he?

Mark: Ah, a question very well put! And the answer of course, is no. I can't believe that Jesus did anything in order to amaze -- nor to amuse -- the throngs, even though one of the most obvious responses was their amazement.

When I was writing, I had included four of Jesus' parables, a good sampling; and then the idea of a sampling of his miracles began to push forward in my thoughts. They were a vitally important part of his ministry. How could I present them in a way to show how significant they were? As I meditated on their significance I began to think of all the sorts of things where ordinary people are powerless. I came up with a short list of four areas.

1. *Power over the Natural Elements*

First, we are powerless over the natural elements: things such as great storms and their effects, such as wind and tempests at sea. So as the first of the four, I sensed that the Spirit was moving me to show that his power was great over these natural elements.

> On that day, when evening had come, he said to them, "Let us go across to the other side."
>
> And leaving the crowd, they took him with them in the boat, just as he was. And other boats were with him. And a great windstorm arose, and the waves were

breaking into the boat, so that the boat was already filling. But he was in the stern, asleep on the cushion. And they woke him and said to him, "Teacher, do you not care that we are perishing?"

And he awoke and rebuked the wind and said to the sea, "Peace! Be still!" And the wind ceased, and there was a great calm. He said to them, "Why are you so afraid? Have you still no faith?" And they were filled with great fear and said to one another, "Who then is this, that even the wind and the sea obey him?" (Mark 4:35-41)

Anyone who reads this account can put himself or herself into one of the two viewpoints that appear. Do you see it from the viewpoint of Jesus, calm, serene, and unconcerned? If so, you can also believe that the twelve disciples were overreacting and too frantic. But then you remember that several of these men were fishermen on that very body of water, and they knew the signs of a storm much more violent than the usual, with high waves breaking over the gunwales so that the boat was beginning to fill with water; and if these experienced boatsmen were concerned to the point of being frantic then this may not have been overreaction at all.

If you read the story from the perspective of the disciples, then you wonder why it took so much of their effort and anxiety to awaken Jesus. Why wasn't he more alert to the situation? And when you take into account the boating and water skills that were represented by at least four of the men in the boat, you understand again that this was a most desperate situation. The wind howled, the waves were high, and the boat was shipping water, *filling* with water. The disciples rightly were powerless against the elements.

When they woke Jesus, did they actually expect he would be able to do anything about their predicament? Or did they only want him to be awake so he could be as alarmed as they were? Their response to his power over nature shows that they were amazed to the greatest extreme: "they feared a great fear" is the way I expressed it in my writing, so when we ask the question whether they expected Jesus to be able to solve the issue, our answer can only be a definite *maybe*.

How much they hoped he might be able to do, not even Peter could tell me. Jesus' authority over wind and waves was not the solution they expected. The disciples were still *learners*, and they had to be constantly adjusting their understanding of who Jesus is, in the complete picture. Jesus showed clearly that even when he was immensely tired in body he still could take command over the fiercest powers of nature.

Background: Miracles in the Old Testament

Here is something that not many people have thought about. From a later point of view it seems as though miraculous events were popping up all the time. Yet when you read everything in its own context it becomes plain that miracles do not appear in the Bible very often at all; and when they do they cluster around certain famous people and around certain fairly definite periods. The people involved are well known to us, both in our apostolic times and in your modern 21st century. They are known both to religious people and beyond, and naturally that's partly because of the miracles. the people are Moses, Joshua, Elijah and Elisha, and much later, Daniel. In addition to the miracles associated with these five men, there were remarkable heroic exploits by Gideon, Samson, David, and Samuel, and some remarkable interpretation of dreams by Joseph, all of these clearly with God's help. Miracles are rare anywhere else in the Old Testament Scriptures -- rare from the time of Daniel until the time of Jesus, when suddenly they become frequent.

Questioner: Mark, you said you had a sequence of examples to mention that demonstrate Jesus' authority, or his power. I think you've given just one, his power over the forces of nature. I take it there are more?

Mark: Yes, I was just ready to tell about the second one.

2. *Jesus' Power Over Demons -- forces of evil*

It happened on the same day, just after Jesus stilled the storm. On the eastern shores of the sea, where most of the people are non-Jewish, Jesus and the twelve were met by a man whose condition was so unusual that most people found him grotesque, and considered him dangerous. He was possessed by a demon, or maybe dozens of demons. He lived in a burial-ground among the tombs, and people were afraid of him. This man had tremendous physical strength, and every attempt to bind him or even to chain him ended in his forceful escape. He seldom had a rational thought, and aside from living among the tombs he was constantly bruising himself with stones.

Surprisingly, when Jesus commanded the spirit to come out of him, the man spoke with knowledge beyond his own: "what have you to do with me, Jesus, Son of the Most High God?" Then he tried to command Jesus' actions with an oath -- "I adjure you by God, do not torment me." But who was speaking -- the man, or the demonic presence that was in possession of his will and his personality? That soon becomes clear, in the words, "my name is Legion, for we are many," using the Latin word representing 6,000 soldiers in the army of Rome.

So, Questioner, some readers of your own times have supposed that this man merely suffered from mental illness and delusion, and that there were no demons or evil spirits. It may be hard for modern people who are trained in finding scientific explanations for everything, to even imagine unseen beings that represent an evil force, even affecting human lives.

The facts are not consistent with that simplistic approach. The unclean spirits recognized Jesus, and he recognized them. This was not a region Jesus visited often: likely he was never here before; so it is hard to believe that a mentally ill person would have both knowledge of who Jesus is ("Jesus, Son of the Most High God") and perception ("I adjure you by God,") to speak to Jesus in those words. It is more in keeping with the whole account and the times and the population to accept that here Jesus was dealing with spirit-entities. His authority over these evil powers -- whether there was one demon, or a few of them, or thousands, as we might guess from the name "Legion,"-- was unquestioned by the people who knew him best. His power over evil forces is the point.

It is a fact, an unfortunate fact, that there were evil forces all around Jesus, trying to undo the good he was doing. The evil sometimes took the form of demonic beings who came to people, intent on making evil out of any goodness within them. At other times it took the form of contesting for the soul of a person, as Satan did at the very beginning of Jesus' mission. Sometimes it took other forms. One of the enemy's greatest schemes is to capture the spirit of an entire organization, even a great organization of political leaders or representatives, such as a council, a sanhedrin, a caucus, or a congress. Is it still the same in your day, Questioner?

Questioner: Yes, Mark, I'm afraid that not much has changed since the days of Jesus' earthly mission. We may have different forms in our government, we may call things by different names, and we may have very different ways of getting news or current events into the hands of people, but it does seem that there are evil forces that make right thinking and right acting seem outmoded and foolish, and that make the new seem true. Even when everyone knows just what happened there seems always to be some other account, by a smooth, persuasive person who says in essence, "what are you going to believe -- me, or your lying eyes?" There must be an element of evil, whether personalized or general, when so many people can be easily persuaded to refuse what their God-given rational minds tell them is right, and stubbornly hold to the wrong in spite of facts.

But we were discussing the power and authority of Jesus over the forces of evil, weren't we? Hm-m-m, I guess we aren't so far off the subject after all, are we, Mark?

You're focusing pretty narrowly on this one incident, Mark. Yet I recall that this isn't the only time in your Gospel that you've written about Jesus casting out demons -- and you've highlighted the authority that he gave to the twelve disciples over demons, too. The risen Christ expects us to bring problems of evil under the power of God in our day and time too, right?

Mark: Right. We who follow Christ, whether in the first century or the twenty-first, may not have all the powers that he had in the time of his public ministry in Galilee and Judea, but he is alive, and he still has power over evil; and if we have access to him, there may be greater power available than we realize.

Questioner: This may be one of the areas where Christians are too cautious, unwilling to take risks in order to make great gains in the cause that Christ came for. But it seems as though it must have been so easy for Christ to have confidence that demons would be submissive to his power. Do you have any advice to give us, Mark?

Mark: As a matter of fact, I do have some advice, and it's a lesson I learned the hard way. You see, my older cousin was called Barnabas, and he was an early traveling missionary, along with Paul. They were very earnest about their task, and my cousin invited me to go along. He thought I would gain valuable experience on the journey, and I'm sure he expected me to catch on, and then to be useful to them and maybe even helpful to new Christians in several ways.

Things went along pretty well for a while, but after only a couple of weeks I thought I was in over my head, and I didn't want to go any further, so from Perga in Pamphylia I turned back alone and returned to Jerusalem. Afterward I had serious feelings of discouragement and defeat, knowing that I had let both of them down, and had earned a prominent place on Paul's black list. I was even the cause of the two of them later dissolving their team and going separate ways.

I learned later that Paul and cousin Barnabas ran into serious opposition as they went on without me, from Antioch in Pisidia, to Iconium, Lystra, and Derbe, presenting Christ to Jews and then to Gentiles too. On one occasion Paul was stoned and dragged out of the city, left for dead.

Why do I tell you this? Because we often fail to risk much at all, let alone risking our lives for the truth of the Gospel. I certainly was in that position. My unwillingness to endure hardship, or even discomfort, put me in a position of shame. It is only because of the mercy of God that I have been able to move beyond that shame and that I was granted a second chance at service for the Lord. Not many weeks after they finished the missionary tour that had proved so hazardous, they became concerned about the new believers in Derbe, Lystra, Iconium, and Antioch of Pisidia. As they prepared for the return visit, Barnabas wanted to take me along again, but Paul wasn't willing to risk having someone who might hinder their work. That someone, of course, was me.

The result of this disagreement was that the two missionaries who had worked so well together parted ways. Paul took Silas with him; Barnabas and I went to other regions to declare the truth of the good news of Christ. Most people see this development as the tragic result of Christian disagreement, but look again, and see that there were two very good results. First, instead of one team (Paul and Barnabas) preaching Christ, there were two: Paul and Silas, and Barnabas and me. Second, I had the chance of making a success of going into the face of some danger and seeing God's protection and his blessing of the effort. Later, as you know, I was able to be helpful to Peter as he traveled even further with the Gospel.

An even more powerful impact on me personally, was the later endorsement of Paul, when he wrote from his imprisonment in Rome to the believers at Colossae: "*Aristarchus my fellow prisoner greets you, <u>and Mark the cousin of Barnabas</u> (concerning whom you have received instructions—if he comes to you, welcome him), and Jesus who is called Justus. These are the only men of the circumcision among my fellow workers for the kingdom of God, and <u>they have been a comfort to me</u>.*" (Colossians 4:10-11) This is not to my credit, it's through the strength that Christ gives, but because I was shamefully timid early on, I resolved to be as bold as any situation would call for, no matter the cost.

Questioner: You haven't put it in these terms, Mark, but I wonder if you weren't doing battle with evil forces yourself. This is a pretty good reminder that we all have our own versions of that battle to fight.

At the bottom line, though, because through your words we can see Jesus casting out demons and dealing with other forces of evil it encourages us to oppose demonic activity and to approach evil boldly, is that it?

Mark: ... to approach evil boldly, yes, but cautiously, and relying on Christ.

Questioner: I'm interested in hearing more of what you have to say about the miracles of Jesus. You said that Jesus demonstrated his power in four different areas through miracles. Could you review for us, so we can see just where we've been and where we're going?

Mark: Glad to. I started describing them just a bit ago with this unbroken sequence of four miracles. They're all found from the end of chapter 4 to the end of chapter 5, in this order. (4:35-5:43)

1. Jesus stilled the storm. Power over nature, over natural forces.

2. "Legion." Jesus cast out demons from the Gerasene demoniac. Power over evil powers and unclean spirits.

The two that are yet to come are these:

3. The woman with a flow of blood cured. Power over illness and disability.

4. Jairus' daughter restored to life. Power over physical death.

3. *Jesus' power over illness and disease*

Normally when Jesus performed a miracle it flowed naturally as the events and circumstances of a day unfolded. When Jesus, James, and John came home with Simon and Andrew after the Sabbath day's service at the synagogue, they found that Simon's mother-in-law was sick in bed, with a fever. When they told Jesus about her illness, he stepped into the room, came forward, and took her by the hand, lifting her up; the fever left her so completely that she got up and began to serve them. Another time, a paralyzed man came forcefully to Jesus' attention when his stretcher was let down through the roof, placing him directly in front of Jesus. So whenever needs came to his attention, these or other healing miracles were performed.

This one incident was very different. On this one occasion the healing sneaked up on him from behind -- literally! It came about after Jesus and the twelve had again crossed the sea from Gerasa, where Jesus had exorcised the "legion" of demons. You know the story well by this time, but let me repeat, with a purpose in mind.

As often happened he was met with a request for healing, this time by a Jewish synagogue official in behalf of his daughter who was critically ill. While Jesus and Jairus were on the way to Jairus' home, Jesus suddenly stopped --

"Who touched my clothing just now?"

With a throng of people pressing around him, the correct answer would be "many people." Yet Jesus was really interested in just one person, the one who had touched him in faith and had received healing. He knew this had happened, because he felt power go forth out of him.

Questioner: What a feeling that must have been! In reading your account, Mark, it has seemed that Jesus had an unlimited amount of power to heal and to perform other amazing works. Here, in the words of Jesus himself, he seems to acknowledge that his power is available in a limited or finite quantity, and he is sensitive to its use.

Mark: Yes, and though as I wrote I didn't need to have full explanations of everything Jesus said, I did feel compelled to present accurately what he said. At about the same time that Jesus felt the power go out from him, the woman felt in her body that she was healed. Her hemorrhage had suddenly ceased, and she knew it. She had heard much about Jesus' power, and in her faith she reasoned that if she could only get close enough to touch his garment, his power would be applied to her need. Even though the healing had been complete without his hands or his words, as a way of confirming the action he listened to the woman's whole story and then spoke to her: "Daughter, your faith has saved you. Go in peace and be healed of your disease." (5:34)

4. *Jesus' Power over Death*

Now you may think it's about time for me to stop and say. "So, where were we?" -- because of course you've noticed that I began to tell about the synagogue official Jairus and his daughter, who was at death's door, but as Jesus and the distraught father were on the way to Jairus' house they were interrupted by the woman who pushed her way close enough to touch Jesus' clothing. I haven't lost my way in the story, because this is the way it happened. But then what happened to Jairus' daughter? Here is the rest of the story, in two parts:

1. *He didn't accept the end of the story*

Before Jesus and Jairus were free to continue their walk to Jairus' house they were met by some people from the synagogue official's house, bearing bad news: "it's too late -- the young girl is now dead," and asking, "Why trouble the teacher any longer?"

That could have been the end of the story. It would have been, too, except for the compassion and power of Jesus. The Lord did not accept her death, and reversed the irreversible.

2. *How do you make mourners laugh?*

Jesus, even before they approached Jairus' home, ignored the dismal message of the friends of the official, and he said to Jairus "do not fear: only believe." He took only Peter, James, and John along with the girl's father and himself. Passing by the sobbing family members and ignoring as much as possible the wailing and weeping of the neighbors, they entered the house and went directly into the room where the lifeless body of the girl was laid.

There were many mourners gathered around, even in the house, and Jesus prepared them for what he knew he was about to do by asking them why the great noise of mourning, since, he said, the child was not dead but asleep. The mourners laughed at him: they knew death when they saw it, and they had quickly gathered from around the neighborhood. Maybe they had been there keeping a vigil before she died, or perhaps most of them had gathered as the news of her death had spread. He requested that they all leave the house and wait outside, then he took the parents and the three disciples who had come along, and they went into the chamber where the girl's body was. He took her by the hand and said two simple words in the Aramaic language: "Talitha coumi," *little one, you can get up now.*

Without delay the girl got up and walked around the room, healthy and hungry as any other twelve-year-old. I don't often seek to carry the message of incidents in the life of Jesus further than the factual description, but let me speculate here just a bit. The little girl was intensely sick, to the point of death. Then because of a delay, she died before Jesus could arrive. He was able to restore her life, and through his power she was also healed from her deadly disease. But in the process he did not free her from hunger: he told her father and mother to give her something to eat.

So my observation is this -- when we see people who receive help from the Lord, we can be amazed at his power and grace and even miracles, and still there are needs for nourishment and care. That remaining task is for his followers to do.

Well, there you have it, the four miracles in sequence, and one sample of each one of the *only four* kinds of miracles that there can be.

Power over nature
Power over forces of evil (Satan and
 demonic forces)
Power over sickness
Power over death

Questioner: Wow -- very interesting, Mark. I've learned that you have so much to offer; this is a bit off the topic of miracles, but I am amazed at how carefully everything fits together. So I'd like to ask you to make a comment or two about the writing process itself. First, did you feel that you were at all free to select material, that is teachings, miracles, and other events in Jesus' life? Or was it all presented to you as a done deal, with no choices left to make on your part?

Mark: Ah, questioner, this is an interesting question, and this may be the best time to say a few words about it, though first I may want to answer a question that you didn't ask. That is the question "why you, Mark?"

In answer to that question: I felt a compulsion to write, but this compulsion didn't seem to come in any ordinary way. Here's how it happened.

I didn't consider myself a writer in any usual sense, but the impulse to write was a response to another kind of need. Peter was a fisherman and boatman, and he sensed strongly that his primary mission was to preach about the Messiah to the Jews. Since boats and fishing were his strong suit, rather than move randomly from town to town, he decided to make the itinerary a regular tour from one fishing village to another, though not missing some of the larger cities inland.

Then, after Peter and I had traveled to all the coastal towns that had Jewish synagogues, we were by that time along the coast of Italy, and he decided to go inland to the Imperial City, Rome. While we were there, we began to find many people who had heard a little preaching or teaching (or even some information passed along on the grapevine) about the Way.

Many of these people had no knowledge of Judaism, but based on what they had heard they were eager to become followers. Their knowledge was quite meager, and it seemed to me that Peter could continue to teach in small public settings, and *someone* had to take up the task of setting down in writing the necessary things about Jesus.

When it became clear that these non-Jewish people in Rome needed a greater understanding of God and of Jesus the Messiah, I simply didn't feel free to avoid this task. Clearly God had been preparing me to do it, for even though I was not one of the Twelve, and I had not even been a follower during most of the Lord's time of ministry, but I'd had those several later years of close association with Peter, and I had heard him tell his stories about Jesus many times. This gave me a large fund of knowledge, direct from the apostle himself.

Questioner: Okay, so you did feel that you were the one person who was especially prepared, and I hear you saying that God had been making you ready, through ample information that came to you by listening to Peter's preaching and teaching, and being his interpreter. So now back to the other part of the question I raised, and that is whether you felt you had any freedom at all in selection of materials?

Mark: I included about twenty accounts of miracles in my writing. I understand that some years after I wrote, the apostle John included only seven of Jesus' miraculous works -- and as he came near the end of his Gospel account he said, "Now Jesus did many other signs in the presence of the disciples, which are not written in this book..." (John 20:30) And then in the very final words of his account he wrote this: "But there are also many other things that Jesus did; if all of them were written one by one I suppose the world itself could not contain the books that would be written." (John 21:25)

John said it well for all of us. There were so many dramatic events to include, they seemed to be competing with each other. I know it seems strange to personalize actual events like that, but during the time I was writing I came to know so many of the events in Jesus' life almost as a man might know his close neighbors, and all of them had something to teach about Jesus.

Yet in the end I not only knew that I was limited in what I could include, but also that each of the miracles that appeared in the writing had to contribute something new to the reader's understanding of Jesus. Remember that when I wrote, I had my *first* readers in mind -- people in the city of Rome, mostly Gentiles, who had heard very little or nothing at all about Jesus. For them, nearly everything would be new, and especially because of this fact nothing untrue, nothing unimportant, nothing misleading should be included.

Back now to your question. Was I free to select stories or episodes to include? It isn't easy to know how many of our decisions are made with added guidance from above. For example, Questioner, how did you decide what questions to ask me? Were they all just hatched from your own curiosity, or were you pretty well informed by previous thinking? Or were you influenced by questions you have heard in conversation, or a class setting? Or was your choice of topics maybe nudged in a certain direction by the Holy Spirit? As for my selection of miracle stories or other events or teachings, I can tell you this much -- I didn't feel as though I was compelled to include or exclude any particular item. I don't think it is an exaggeration to say that I have heard of a hundred miracles or so that center on Jesus. But these twenty accounts, added to the three summary references just seemed to tell the whole story of Jesus' power. So, whether I was free to make those choices or not, however much God influenced my thinking and my selection, I *felt* free, and at the same time I felt that these miracles were the right ones.

Questioner: Well, how does this impact the idea of the inspiration of Scripture?

Mark: I firmly believe in the inspiration and authority of all Scripture, but during the process of my writing it wasn't clear to me yet that anything I wrote was destined to be included in the Scriptures. God's purposes often become much clearer afterward, as we look back on them.

Besides, what God wanted me to write for the Gentile people of Rome continued to be helpful and useful for many other people. It was soon shared with other communities throughout the Roman Empire. From there it continued on down through many generations, even down to your own times in the 21st century. I couldn't have foreseen that, but God continues to use it to introduce people to Christ.

Questioner: Thank you, Mark. I'm glad for your reflection on that. Another question, before we move on beyond the subject of miracles -- we've already looked into the purpose of miracles, and

I've agreed with you that they are a demonstration of several things.

> 1. Jesus had such *compassion* for those in need that he just *had* to help.
> 2. That God is affirming, or confirming the truth of Jesus' words by miraculous *signs*.
> 3. They dramatically show the power of Jesus over *nature*, over *evil and demons*, over *disease*, and over *death*.

So, Mark, do you think that there other reasons that miracles were such a frequent part of the ministry of Jesus?

Mark: Yes, I do. Here are a few more thoughts on the question why Jesus' ministry is known for his miraculous acts. I'll just add these four items to your numbered list.

> 4. The miracles show us time and again which side he is on. He taught often in his words about the Kingdom of God; his miracles are a demonstration in action of that Kingdom. The miracles *show the Kingdom opening up* in the present age for people like us who are limited too much by the world we can see, so the mighty acts of Christ become a glimpse of the realities of the world we're destined for.
> 5. They also show us a *payback, or reward*, for faith.

6. Sometimes, possibly, they even *confirmed to Jesus himself* that the way he was following was the exact way God wanted him to go.

7. As Son of God he was *so full of power* that miraculous acts and events just came from him like drops of water drip off your fingers after you dip them into a bucket of water.

Before we go on to another subject, I think it would be a good idea to have a list of the miracles as they appear in my account of the Gospel. You'll find twenty specific miracles, along with three summaries of miracle occasions. These summaries are marked with an asterisk.

ACCOUNTS OF MIRACLES IN MARK

1. Demon cast out in Synagogue in Capernaum 1:23-27
2. Simon's Mother-in-law Cured of a fever 1:30-31
3. *Many Cured at Evening 1:32-34
4. A Leper cleansed 1:40-45
5. Paralyzed Man Healed in Capernaum 2:1-12
6. Man With a Withered Hand Healed 3:1-5
7. *Many Healed and Demons Cast Out 3:9-12
8. Jesus Stilled the Storm 4:35-41
9. Demons Cast Out of "Legion" Demoniac at Gerasa 5:1-20
10. The Bleeding Woman 5:25-34
11. The Daughter of Jairus 5:22-24, 35-43
12. A Few sick people healed at Nazareth 6:5
13. Feeding the 5,000 6:31-44
14. Jesus Walked on Water 6:45-52
15. *Many Healings at Gennesaret 6:53-56
16. Syrophoenician woman's daughter cured of demon 7:24-30
17. Curing a Deaf and Mute Man 7:31-37
18. Feeding the 4,000 8:1-10
19. Healing a Blind Man at Bethsaida 8:22-26
20. The Transfiguration of Jesus 9:2-8
21. Cure of Demon-possessed Boy 9:14-29
22. Bartimaeus receives his sight 10:46-52
23. Jesus Cursed a Fig Tree 11:12-14, 20-22

* These three times the account says many were cured, with no specific examples given.

Chapter 14
Parables

Parables as Puzzles

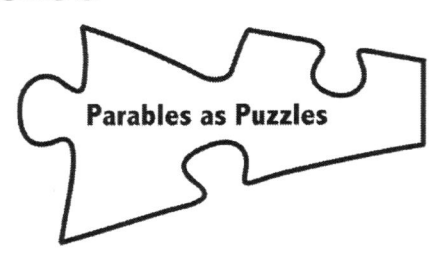

Questioner: Mark, in the previous chapter I felt that we were digging in and exploring the heart of Jesus' purpose and ministry. In particular, when you tied the miracles in as mighty acts reinforcing Jesus' strong emphasis on the Kingdom of God, it made it apparent that there was a higher and larger purpose for the miracle-work Jesus did. I don't want to let that thought get lost in the midst of everything else you've been helping us to see.

Now I want to ask you about the *Parables* of Jesus. I guess everybody knows that Jesus taught by using parables. I've watched for them, especially because of these words that you wrote after you concluded a very short section on parables:

> With many such parables he used to speak the word to them, fitted to their ability to understand; he did not speak to them without a parable, but privately to his own followers he spelled everything out. (4:33-34)

This sentence is a comment, written directly to the readers of your account. It just pops up there in the flow of the narrative, and it comes just after a short series of parables (a list of *four*, naturally). Earlier you mentioned that a Gospel is similar to portraying the action like a stage play: where the playwright is not in view, but merely opening the curtain for the audience; but this would be more like the playwright stepping onto the stage to explain something to the audience -- not completely unknown in drama, but not the usual style in a play.

I have several questions about parables, but one of my big questions, Mark, is this: in your own comment you put great emphasis on Jesus' teaching in parables, and from everything else we hear about Jesus we can be confident that he taught regularly in this style. So why did you include so little of his parable-teaching? I think you included only about 49 verses of parable -- only about 7% of your Gospel writing. With phrases like "with many similar parables he spoke the word to them ... and without a parable he did not speak to them," we somehow get the feeling that we may be missing out on quite a bit.

Your sentence makes me pause. There are only four parables here in chapter four, contained in just eighteen verses. I've looked carefully in other places in your Gospel account and found several parables-- though not nearly as many as I would expect to find, based on your comment I just quoted. In addition to these four parables in chapter four, on the list just above, there is only one other long parable, *The Evil Tenant-Farmers*, (12:1-12), and three shorter ones.

Mark: Yes, "Q" (By now maybe I should call you by just your initial. I hope I'm not being too familiar). I had a reason for this, a few reasons, actually.

As I begin to wonder about how to answer you, I realize that there are several questions here, or at least one question with several parts. You think that there's a contradiction in my way of presenting Jesus and his teaching in parables. If I wasn't planning to re-tell many of the parables, why did I say "and he did not speak to them without a parable," or on the other hand if I said that he *always* used them, why didn't I include more of them?

Reason one: A Sample Tells a Story Larger Than Itself

When we were just now looking at the miracles of Jesus, you recall that a few times I described Jesus healing a person with a touch, or sometimes not even touching the person, and then for later examples of the same sort of miracles I freely summarized ["for he had healed many, so that whoever had diseases pressed in to touch him, and whenever the unclean spirits beheld him they fell down before him and cried out, 'You are the Son of God." (3:10-11)].

When I explained the principles I followed in describing the *miracles* in Jesus' ministry, it was easy for you to see the *summaries* that I included of his healings, and times when he cast out unclean spirits, and I think it helps to tell the story of Jesus and his ministry if we don't include every detail. Something like that became my reason for giving samples of the parables he told, without trying to report all of them. A sample often tells a story larger than itself.

Reason two: Economy of Writing Materials, Size, and Time

In very many ways you live in a very favored time. In your era large quantities of paper and writing materials are available at very low cost, so for you this part may be a bit difficult to grasp. In my times everything was written on vellum or papyrus, both very expensive.

Vellum was a very fine, nearly-white writing surface, but it had to be prepared from the untanned skins of a sheep, goat, or calf. The process was expensive in time and materials: It had to be cleaned, de-haired and scraped, then stretched and dried. After it was stretched, it was polished with pumice, which is a fine abrasive, and talc, to fill tiny imperfections, as a final preparation for writing. In my age only the most official documents, ones intended to survive for centuries, were produced on vellum.

The other choice for writing was papyrus. It was much cheaper than vellum, probably about one tenth as expensive. The way to produce a sheet of papyrus was to go to a marsh or the bank of a stream or river, and gather a cart-load of reeds of the *papyrus* plant. Then you transport them the distance, sometimes close but often many miles, to the place of production -- I'll call it the paper factory. The reeds you have gathered grow from two to five feet high, and have a hard surface all the way around the length of the reed stem, a sort of "bark." Carefully strip this bark off, and keep the pithy inside, then cut it into narrow strips about a foot long. Lay these strips parallel to each other, then lay another set on top, perpendicular to them, and begin to pound them with a mallet. This process fuses them together, and with time, effort, and patience you will have a sheet of papyrus ready to be cut to size and filled with the written word.

The process, whether done by you, or me, or even a very low-wage worker, is pretty intensive in terms of the labor and skill involved, so *a single sheet* of material for writing would, in your modern terms, cost in the neighborhood of $10.00 to possibly $20.00. For a scroll of very modest size it could cost up to three to five hundred dollars. That's for just one copy! Maybe you can begin to understand one reason for economy in recording Jesus' parables.

Questioner: As I think about it, a larger scroll would not have been nearly as easy to carry and share, and it would have taken much longer to write.

Mark: Besides, do you sense that there is a lot of important information missing from my Gospel? Once more we can think about the words from another Gospel: There are many other things that Jesus did "...*that are not written here. But these are written so that you can believe that Jesus is the Christ, the Son of God.*" (John 20:30-31)

Questioner: Mark, it's one of those famous "facts" that everybody seems to know, that the reason Jesus taught with the use of parables was to make his point plain. Naturally, you've included several parables in your Gospel account. Though some of them are very easy to understand, some others don't seem easy, they seem more like *puzzles*. Maybe you could help me understand these difficulties. But before you help us with that, I'd like to sum up some observations that I have about parables, and I have a couple of more basic questions to ask about parables, too.

1. Chapter 4 of your Gospel is known as the chapter on parables, with most of this chapter dedicated to just four of Jesus' parables and two additional parts that closely relate to them. Three of these four parables incorporate the idea of seed and growth; and the other one (second in the sequence) is a very brief rhetorical question about the placement of a lamp -- on a stand, and not under a basket or under the bed.

(1) the Parable of the Sower and the Soils (4:3-9) The disciples are puzzled.

- Next you have a short, puzzling saying on the reason for parables (4:10-12)

- Then Jesus' very clear interpretation of the parable on the Sower -- no puzzle here. (4:13-20)

(2) the Parable of the Lamp under a Basket (4:21-25)

(3) the Parable of the Seed that Sprouts and Grows until harvest (4:26-29)

(4) the Parable of the Mustard Seed (4:30-32).

(5)- In addition to this short section on parables in your fourth chapter, there are those few very short ones in your Gospel in other locations.

a) The Fig Tree, 13:28-31

b) The Watchful Servants, 13:33-37

c) A kingdom divided against itself, 3:23-27

Then also you include a few even shorter imaginative references, sometimes only a few words long. I've heard these called "little images." They're allusions so brief that only rarely would people include them among the parables. I happen to have a list of them, so I'll name them here.

a) a patched garment (2:21)

b) new wineskins for new wine (2:22)

c) the measure you give will be the measure you get (4:24)

d) the bridegroom taken away (2:19-20)

Now, here is a question that I've never known anyone to ask. *Is there a parable in 8:19-21?*

By the time of that event Jesus has performed two very similar miracles: the two miracle feedings -- the first one was received by 5,000 people, and the second one by 4,000. The food at the beginning of the first was 5 loaves and for the other, 7 loaves; the unneeded leftovers were twelve baskets and seven hampers, and shortly afterward Christ faced his followers with a puzzling question, "do you not yet understand?"

Obviously in reviewing the basic facts and making the disciples identify the quantity of left over fragments, Jesus is trying to get the twelve to stumble onto some great truth. Mark, I wonder if we treat this event, the disciples and Jesus crossing the sea without food provisions as *an enacted parable*, can we examine the questions that Jesus asks the twelve, and watch for deeper meanings? Deeper meanings are obviously there. Jesus makes it clear that he wants the disciples to stretch their minds to remember what they have experienced in his presence and to put the event together with what he has said. His teaching began with a warning about the "leaven" (or yeast) of the Pharisees and the leaven of Herod.

Mark: If you can stretch your understanding of what should be considered a parable in my Gospel, you should follow the dialogue carefully. The disciples weren't perceptive, and Jesus even asked them if their hearts were hardened. There are several "layers" of meaning.

Simply put, the *first layer* is the warning against the leaven (corruption) that the Pharisees and Herod had in common. Not only had the Pharisees conspired together with people who were partisans of Herod (called *Herodians*) to destroy Jesus (so lesson one: watch out for what these people can do to you!) but both of these kinds of people were out for themselves first (don't be *like* them, either!).

The *second layer* is easy, too: these men were in a boat, and they had only one small loaf of bread, and they had Jesus. If he could feed 5,000 people with five loaves, or 4,000 with seven, how hard would it be for him to feed only 13 people with one loaf? Piece of cake, right?

The *third layer* of meaning is a bit trickier. Jesus asks pointedly how many baskets of fragments were left over. He forces the twelve to think about the abundance -- the over-supply when he is involved. He wants them to notice the *amount* of over-abundance.

When he feeds 5,000 with 5 loaves, 12 baskets.
When he feeds 4,000 with 4 loaves, 7 baskets.

If we understand that the first miracle was in a Jewish setting and location, and that the *fives* and *twelves* are Jewish symbolic numbers, then we look and find *four* and *seven* prominent and we remember that these are *whole-world* numbers (the four winds; the four corners of the earth; and seven even in the Old Testament often standing for inclusiveness and totality).

So at the *third level* of understanding we can apply the truth that Jesus means that the good news should be carried by his followers not only to their own people, but to those beyond: to the entire world *and there will still be abundance!*

This brings us back to where Jesus began: beware of the *corruption* of the Pharisees and Herod -- which is not only hypocrisy, and not only opposition to Jesus and his disciples, but even deeper: it is a deep corruption to *keep the good news for yourselves*. The life-changing message of God's forgiveness and his blessing is for the whole world!

So even though this event really happened, that the disciples *had* forgotten to bring bread, Jesus built on the event as a complex parable, and applied deeper and richer meaning to it.

Questioner: Then, Mark, when we think about parables should we also include the very brief saying about the millstone (9:42), cutting off parts of the body (9:43-48)? Also, there is the time in the final week of Jesus' life when he cursed the fig tree (11:12-14, 21) These are comparisons, and they hold serious warnings that no earnest follower can afford to ignore.

What are the marks of a parable?

1. It will have meaning on more than one level.

2. It will use symbolic language -- one thing or person is a symbol for another.

3. The natural level is recognizable as allowing its "other" meaning. (The seed that fell among thorns has an obvious point. We can all imagine some thorns that would choke out the good Word of God.)

4. It will enlist the hearers on the right side, so we give it our willing acceptance. (We would not put the candle or lamp under the bed, oh, no!)

5. We can learn by this good, or that bad example: There is a Good Samaritan, and an uncaring Levite. We learn from both of them.

6. Most parables have room for "me," that is, the person who hears the parable or reads it should be able to picture himself or herself in the situation (for example, the sower, the patch, the wineskins, or the doorkeeper). But this isn't true of all of them, such as the seed growing by itself, or the mustard seed, the tenants, fasting.

7. Are parables like allegories? No, they are comparisons of familiar things, and often of

familiar kinds of people, good and bad. Allegories have sequential development of story or action, with separate meanings for each part.

8. Is the point obvious? Yes, usually, and often the point is made even more explicit by Jesus. But there is this one thing to watch out for: Mark will sometimes leave the parable in the style of a puzzle.

9. Is there only "one main point"? (Some other scholars say so, but carry this idea too far, and make it a rule without leaving room for application of some of the longer parables such as the parable of the Sower/Soils.)

10. The most important point is that parables present very important spiritual concepts, and even duties or commands, through ordinary, everyday comparisons.

Is "earthly story with a heavenly meaning" a good definition??

They are earthly stories, for sure. Most often, they are just commonsense reminders, placed next to the thing they want to teach: *this* is like *that*.

- New wineskins for new wine: My Kingdom cannot be fitted into the old forms, the old confines.

- But isn't the Patch parable the opposite truth? Don't sew a new patch on an old garment? Or is the teaching "get a new garment -- one that doesn't need to be patched"? If we get a sense of familiarity of the meaning of parables it helps us to see the inner message of what Jesus was teaching.

Mark: The teaching of Jesus was not always gentle and mild. Another side of his teaching is expressed, for one example, in the parable of the Tenants (12:1-10). Don't fail to notice also this interesting series of nuggets containing his stern advice to all his followers:

> *Whoever causes one of these little ones who believe in me to sin, it would be better for him if a great millstone were hung around his neck and he were thrown into the sea.*
> *And if your hand causes you to sin, cut it off. It is better for you to enter life crippled than with two hands to go to hell, to the unquenchable fire.*
> *And if your foot causes you to sin, cut it off. It is better for you to enter life lame than with two feet to be thrown into hell.*
> *And if your eye causes you to sin, tear it out. It is better for you to enter the kingdom of God with one eye than with two eyes to be thrown into hell....* (9:42-47)

Since Jesus "did not speak to them without a parable," we could try to explain each of these, the millstone, the removal of hand, foot, eye, as parables: some of them are verbal illustrations, included for dramatic effect. The millstone, for example, shows us how solemn is our responsibility toward the "little ones who believe" in Christ.

Questioner: Mark, the words of Jesus in your ninth chapter immediately following the warning about the millstone is the saying about cutting off your hand or your foot, or plucking out an eye if it causes you to sin. Jesus makes it clear that these reasons for stumbling aren't excuses to hide behind. They are a grave, serious matter. Even so, no matter how earnestly we take the warning itself, it is still hard to imagine anyone taking it so literally as actually to mutilate himself or herself in any of these ways.

The bottom line though, is this: if you or I, or any believer commits a sin, what is the cause? Where can we place the blame? Is it the foot that caused it? The hand? The eye? Mark, in your seventh chapter, along with Jesus' authoritative pronouncement about traditions concerning other things such as food, or failing to observe a ritual or ceremonial sprinkling, Jesus ruled out the hand or foot or eye as causes of defilement: "For from within, out of the heart of the person come evil thoughts; fornication, theft, murder, adultery [and eight more kinds of sinfulness and offense against God and other people]." Continuing to quote Jesus, "All these evil things come from within...." (8:21-23)

Mark: You see then, that these sayings are serious warnings, warnings put in vivid terms so we can easily picture the case they make -- but your question still is, *are they parables*?

Questioner: Yes -- and are parables puzzles in disguise? I have often thought that the common description of the parable as "an earthly story with a heavenly meaning" wasn't very appropriate, especially for your Gospel. It seems to fit well for Luke. In Matthew they tend to be earthly stories that tell how God judges. And then in your Gospel they have the quality of *puzzles* to be solved, or discerned, to help us see things as God sees them.

Mark, even if we can see that parables have some of the flavor of puzzles, in the re-telling of the two longest parables in your Gospel you've minimized the "puzzle" aspect by giving the "authoritative interpretation," or the solution. One of the two long parables has Jesus' own guide for interpretation. That's the parable of the seed sown on four kinds of soil, usually known as The Parable of the Sower. Jesus ended that parable with a phrase that he used at other times: "whoever has ears to hear, needs to listen," (4:9, and also in 4:23) or, "whoever has ears to hear, let him hear." [Sometimes Jesus shortens this to just "listen up!" (4:3)]

The other long parable is also accompanied by an interpretation, but this time it is not Jesus who gives the interpretation: this is the parable of the evil tenant-farmers of the vineyard. It ends with the knowledge of the chief priests and the scribes and the elders, when they perceived that Jesus had told the parable with these leaders in mind. With a simple line, only ten words in the English translation, Mark, you've given us the key to understand the parable and its meaning.

It can be an "earthly story with a heavenly meaning," often ending with the destination of heaven or hell. This is especially likely to be the case in Matthew's Gospel.

A parable can be an extended human interest story, a comparison of human choices. This is particularly true of the parables that are found only in Luke.

Mark: Very true. Jesus was not a simple man, though he communicated well to every type of hearer. His parables reflect this, with long and short ones, simple and sublime.

The descriptions you and I have mentioned above deserve one more. A parable also can be just a bit puzzling, with an elusive element. A parable sometimes is an illustration or a story, or even Jesus' reflection on a recent event -- to explore *but not necessarily to explain every aspect* of the truth or reality from God's point of view. I haven't avoided including a bit of puzzle in my Gospel account.

Parables In Mark

When should the wedding guests fast?	2:19-20	Time to rejoice now, mourn later
New cloth used to patch an old garment	2:21	It is so new the old cannot merely be patched
New wine bursts old wineskins	2:22	The Kingdom cannot be contained in old forms
The Kingdom divided against itself	3:23-26	Satan doesn't oppose evil
The strong man's house	3:27	[Who is the strong man?]
The Sower	4:2-9,14-20	God sows the Word: what kind of soil are we?
Lamp under a Basket	4:21-22	Let it shine!
The Growing Seed	4:26-29	God's work will go on: we don't need to know how.
The Mustard Seed	4:30-32	Amazing growth - it's in the DNA
The Causes of Stumbling	9:42-48	Warning! Don't cause others to stumble
The Wicked Tenants	12:1-12	Oppose Christ at your own risk
The Fig Tree	13:28-32	Signs of the end of time
The Watchful Doorkeeper	13:33-37	Servants of God need to watch for God's plan to unfold

Chapter 15

Mark's "Sandwiches"

Questioner: Mark, I have great appreciation for the clear and simple style of your writing. I think it would be easy for any reader to spend even an hour's time with your Gospel account and get the main points of the purpose of Jesus' mission. I'm not the first to notice that you, more than other writers, weave the narrative stories together in layers -- like a sandwich.

One example of this characteristic is the account of one certain day when a worried man named Jairus, one of the officials of the synagogue in Capernaum, appealed to Jesus for help, and while they were on the way to Jairus' house a woman was healed. The sequence is in this passage:

> And when Jesus had crossed again in the boat to the other side, a great crowd gathered about him, and he was beside the sea.
> Then one of the rulers of the synagogue, named Jairus, came and when he saw him, fell at his feet and begged him urgently, saying, "My little daughter is at death's door. Please come and lay your hands on her, so that she may recover, and live." And he went with him.
> And a great crowd followed him and pressed close about him. And there was a woman who had had a discharge of blood for twelve years, and who had suffered much under many physicians,

and had spent all that she had, and was no better but in fact grew worse.

She had heard the reports about Jesus and came up behind him in the crowd and touched his garment. For she said, "If I touch even his garments, I will be made well."And immediately the flow of blood dried up, and she felt in her body that she was healed of her suffering. And Jesus, perceiving in himself that power had gone out from him, immediately turned around in the crowd and said, "who touched my garments?"

And his disciples said to him, "You can see the crowd pressing around you, and yet you say, 'Who touched me?'" And he looked around to see who had done it.

But the woman, knowing what had happened to her, came in fear and trembling and fell down before him and told him the whole truth. And he said to her, "Daughter, your faith has made you well; go in peace, and be healed of your suffering."

While he was still speaking, there came from the ruler's house some who said, "Your daughter is dead. Why trouble the Teacher any further?" But overhearing what they said, Jesus said to the ruler of the synagogue, "Do not fear, only believe." And he allowed no one to follow him except Peter and James and John, who was James' brother.

They came to the house of the ruler of the synagogue, and Jesus saw a commotion, people weeping and wailing loudly. And when he had entered, he said to them, "Why are you making a commotion and weeping? The child is not dead but sleeping." And they laughed at him. But he put them all outside and took the child's father and mother and those who were with him and went in where the child was.

Taking her by the hand he said to her, "Talitha cumi," which means, "Little girl, I say to you, arise." And immediately the girl got up and began walking (for she was twelve years of age), and they were immediately overcome with amazement. And he strictly charged them that no one should know this, and told them to give her something to eat. (5:21-43)

Mark: There are two stories here, connected together. They both are important in their own right, but let me re-tell the incidents the way Jairus might have seen them. Jairus was a worried father who held on to the hope that Jesus could heal his little girl's fearful disease. But it never occurred to him that Jesus could have power over death too. From illness and disease he had seen people recover. But death, never.

Time was of the essence. Jesus got that. The two men started out right away for Jairus' house. But though they didn't have far to go, there were so many people, all coming together in the streets and lanes of Capernaum that it was difficult to pick their way through. Only one thing was important to Jairus. Not his importance, or his professional standing in the town, not the people who came to worship, not even the settled religious opinions that made most of the scribes skeptical of Jesus. *This man is my only chance!*

She's at death's door! Those words kept rolling over in the mind of Jairus, heavier with each repetition. There was a throng of people, and every time someone else stepped in the way, or wouldn't move out of the way they slowed Jairus and Jesus down even more. *Death's door! Why don't these people sense that this is urgent?* Then, as though there was no hurry at all, Jesus suddenly stopped. "Who touched my clothing?" It was all Jairus could do to keep from crying out. His heart was breaking, and this father's hope was interrupted by a woman's fear-filled admission. Then, she just had to tell her story, how she had suffered the painful, debilitating "hemorrhage" for twelve years. She went on and on, about her twelve years of misery and exclusion, and her disappointment with the round of physicians, and the poverty in which they left her. And all this time Jesus didn't seem to hurry; he listened patiently to her. But time was slipping away -- and so was the life of a little girl, who had only been allowed a lifetime of those same twelve years.

Why, oh why, can't he hurry?

Then, before they got away from this woman, two or three people came from Jairus' house to bring him the sad news. "Your daughter has died. No sense in bothering the teacher any more." His eyes brimming with tears, he tried to tell Jesus that it was over; but he could only turn his face away, and weep the tears of despair. *If Jesus had only kept moving -- why did he have to stop there?*

It was hard to understand a man like Jesus. For now that it was too late, against all common sense, Jesus continues to the house. Neighbors who had been watchers and helpers now have become mourners, but Jesus raises a question in their minds about what they are doing there. Then he takes charge and makes the room of her death into a sanctuary for six people: three disciples, two parents, and himself. With a gentle word of command and the touch of his hand, suddenly there aren't six people, but seven. The young girl is brought back through death's door, back into life! She was awake and aware, walking around and eating.

Why are these two accounts sandwiched together? Well, first I would say because they *belong* together. But that isn't really an answer, and it sounds like I'm avoiding the question. I have to admit that I *like* to write with accounts connected together. But there's something more.

When you see this, you should look for some connection between the two stories, where the inner part of the sandwich helps to focus on the significance of the parts that come before and after. Look especially for an opportunity to place yourself into the ideas of the account. Let me spell that out for you.

[It's not only about Jesus -- it's about you]

The *faith* of the woman was strong, though she herself was fearful. The faith of Jairus began strong, and in fact he was bold in his request. But when the sad news reached him, Jesus had to renew him with the words, "do not fear, only believe." Now how do these ideas fit into your life, *our* lives? Faith is often not alone: it may be mingled with fear. But that's a dangerous situation, because faith can be overcome by fear. It's also a hopeful situation, because on the other hand fear can be overcome and defeated by faith. Look again at the woman. Look at Jesus' words. Look at the result in Jairus' house.

If you were going to ask about some other layered accounts, let me just mention the very natural one in the next section, where the twelve disciples were sent out as six pairs of representatives of Jesus to do mission work (6:7-13, 6:30).

They didn't go out and return immediately, so here was a perfect place to place the account of the death of John the Baptist (6:14-29), even though the event itself had happened long before. How does the death of John help us to understand the mission of the twelve? The disciples were sent out to serve, and to serve at the mercy of the people. No weapons, no extra clothing, no financial resources.

In fact, the disciples' equipment (or *lack* of equipment!) was very much like John the Baptist. To serve in the mission of Christ has always been a dangerous challenge, and yes, sometimes it ends, like John's, in martyrdom. Many thousands of missionaries have escaped that fate, but many have not. Many people still remember that I became so fearful on a mission trip with Paul and my cousin Barnabas that I pulled out and abandoned the work. Later I did work with Peter, overcoming my fears. Still it is the quest and the challenge for me. Perhaps also for you.

Questioner: And so you're suggesting that the sandwiched stories are meant to draw us into the action so we, the readers, can make personal application. That's an important point to keep in mind.

Now I want to bring up one sandwich that doesn't seem to fit that pattern. When Jesus cursed the fig tree, and just one day later when he and the disciples passed by it had dried up, withered to its roots (11:12-14, 11:20-22). The event in between the curse and the observation of the result happens in Jerusalem: Jesus entered the temple and drove out those who were making it a den of thieves. So, Mark, do you see a connection between these accounts that I haven't seen?

Mark: Well, yes, actually I do. In the books of the prophets trees are used to symbolize Israel as a nation, and in Jeremiah figs are used as a symbol of Israel -- good figs for the faithful of the nation and "vile" figs for the unfaithful. In Jesus' actions, the curse on the leafy but unfruitful tree and the clearing of dishonest commerce from the very Temple of God, Jesus is calling Israel, his own people, to account. They need to account for the fruitlessness and easy tolerance of evil under their corrupt leaders. I'm sure that the curse is not for every individual -- it covers the national indifference that reigned. It would be less than four days until the crowd would cry out for Jesus to be crucified. Of course there would be many who would resist that plan, but where were they at the crucial moment? Huge crowds with a common voice make cowards of many of us.

The disciples saw that the tree became dried up down to the roots. They marveled at this, but rather than dwelling on the lesson for them, or us, or even the nation, Christ follows up with teachings on the power of prayer and unwavering faith.

You may wonder about the connection. The power of a curse, allied with prayer? or the power of faith and prayer, to counteract a curse? or is it that faith in God and prayer is the only protection from heaven's curse on an evil world? As often, I give you the clues. The puzzle is yours. Your answer will probably depend on how closely you have come to know Jesus, and how much you trust him.

Chapter 16

Can Mark's Gospel be Outlined?

Questioner: Many people seem to have noticed the same thing as they studied your account of the Gospel: that is, it seems incredibly hard to come up with an outline for your work. As you wrote, did you work from any sort of outline? One attempted outline that I have seen for your Gospel account has these broad strokes:

> I. Jesus' Ministry to the Public chapters 1-7
> II. Jesus' Ministry to the Disciples, chapters 8-10
> III. Jesus' Ministry in Jerusalem, chapters 11-16

And another is very similar, but is organized with reference to chronology:

> I. The first three years ... (1-7)
> II. The Next three Months ... (8-10)
> III. The Final Week ... (11-16)

To me, these are not only very unbalanced, they are also not very helpful. Everybody who thinks about it seems to admit that a good outline is very difficult to come up with in your account. So I want to give you an opportunity to respond -- did you have an outline (or at least a sense of organization) in mind as you wrote?

Mark: Outlines differ, and so do the people who devise them. When a person begins a journey, it is helpful if there is a map, and if not then we need to know some *landmarks* along the way. This may not qualify as a map, exactly, but I can offer you some landmarks.

LANDMARK 1:

The Resounding Success in the Early Months

I actually thought in clusters of events as I wrote. Of course I felt compelled to write what I knew about Christ. I believed then, and I still believe, that it was the Spirit of God who energized my mind in the writing process, from beginning to end.

At the beginning I felt that what was needed was the briefest possible introduction, omitting references to Jesus' family, home town, even detailed description of Jesus' temptations. But after the brief reference to his baptism, the very brief acknowledgement of the temptation, and still more brief mention of his preaching, I dashed -- some say 'breathlessly' into a series, a sampling, of the Lord's activities. There was the calling of the first four disciples, then his teaching in the synagogue at Capernaum, an encounter with a demon, healing a woman (Simon's mother-in-law), then many people cured of demons and diseases, his praying alone, and the cure of a man with leprosy. You can watch for other examples of all of these activities in later sections of the account.

LANDMARK 2

Challenges

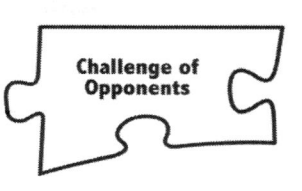

The next section, however, takes a very different approach. In this part there are four times when Jesus is <u>challenged</u> by groups that soon become his opponents. In connection with another healing miracle was a bold claim by Jesus to have the authority to forgive sins. The scribes, who were the professional scholars and guardians of the law, inwardly challenged his claim. To them it was blasphemy that any man would dare to claim that authority.

In the same section Jesus ate with tax collectors, he did not direct his disciples to fast, and he would not restrain his followers from plucking and eating grain, even though it was the Sabbath. Jesus gave replies to their objections, but his answers were not acceptable to the scribes and other officials, because each of these was a violation of the interpretations of the religious leaders.

LANDMARK 3

Opposition

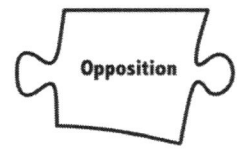

What in the second section we can see as *challenges* become in the next section open *opposition*, by the same people and even some others. The most stark and abrupt part follows my brief reference to Jesus restoring a man's withered hand to wholeness. Some Pharisees were there in the Synagogue watching Jesus closely, suspecting that he might not be able to resist his natural inclination to heal him though it was a Sabbath. Knowing what they were up to, Jesus looked over at them in anger. Two things happened then: he healed the man, and the Pharisees went out and entered into a conspiracy with the Herodians, seeking the best way to destroy Jesus.

This sets the tone for the rest of this section: people who knew him tried to take him away because some said that he was out of his mind (3:21). Some translations say this was his family (a careful and accurate translation would read "those with him went out to seize him"), but this "family" translation is hard to accept because the fourth instance of opposition in this section is his family (3:31-34), involved in a way that shows that they were well-intentioned, yet stood in the way of his calling. There is one other instance of opposition in this section. Scribes, those men who knew and loved to study the Law of the Jewish people, and offer interpretations of it had now come to a conclusion about Jesus: since he was not one of them, and not a Pharisee, nor a Sadducee, nor a representative of the Essenes, yet he had power to cast out demons -- he must have that power from the Devil!

Jesus didn't always answer his opponents, but this time he did. His answer was less about himself and their accusation about him than it was a clarification of which side the devil was on, and a solemn warning to these opponents about their own standing before God. Briefly, his answer was this:

"Think about it: does it make any sense to you that the power of Satan would oppose Satan's own demons? Any kingdom fighting against itself cannot survive for long. And while you're thinking about that, think about how God will judge you. Think about how spiritually dangerous it is for anyone to see the Spirit of God at work and call that the work of the Devil. This is a horrendous sin against God, and the kind of blasphemy that you may never be able to repent of."

Questioner: So this section (chapter 3) has *four* different instances of opposition to Jesus, exactly balancing the *four* challenges to him in the previous section (chapter 2). One further note: when the names of the 12 disciples are listed, the last one in the list was "Judas Iscariot, who betrayed him." (3:19) The mention of the betrayal is completely fitting here in this section where opposition is the main theme, and it's almost a ready-made answer to the "problem" facing the

Pharisees and the Herodians, namely, "how to destroy him" (3:6).

Mark: This may be an interesting fact for you to note: near the end of our Gospel there will be four more challenges, each one from a different powerful group, and each one a difficult question intended to trap Jesus.

Here is the place that Jesus gives replies that disarm the threat of the question: the Pharisees, who hate the very idea of Rome's dominance over Israel, ask: "Is it lawful to pay taxes to Caesar?" Jesus replies, "Give to Caesar the things that are Caesar's, and to God the things that are God's"

The Sadducees, who don't even believe in life after death, ask a complicated hypothetical question about a woman who had outlived seven brothers, each in turn married to her in accord with a directive in Leviticus. Jesus' answer begins, "Your mistake is that you do not understand either the Scriptures or the power of God." The rest of his reply points to an understanding of the Old Testament that they had missed, and in a way that they could not object to.

This later section should remind all of us that determined opposition to him and his mission never went away.

LANDMARK 4

Parables

Mark continues: The next landmark that you will see in my brief guided tour is a section on parables. We have already considered this -- it was not long ago, in fact. Here you have the *four* examples of parables. Before Jesus gave the interpretation of the parable of the four kinds of soil, the disciples asked him about his use of parables in general. His answer at first seems puzzling: "to you has been given the secret of the kingdom of God; but for those outside everything is in parables, so they may see but not perceive, and hear but not understand -- so they will never repent and receive forgiveness."Another rendering of the original words would be, "...but for those outside everything is in parables *with the result that* they will see and hear without understanding, and they will never repent and be forgiven."

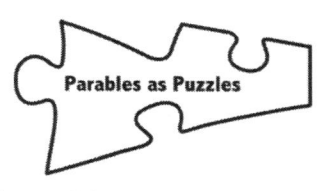

In either way of saying it, it sounds as though there were some people that Jesus did not want to be able to comprehend his words. But often the best way of hearing Jesus is the simplest. Jesus is drawing on a theme found in several places in the Old Testament, and especially in Isaiah 6:9-10

> Keep on hearing but do not understand
> keep on seeing but do not perceive.

> Make the heart of this people dull,
>> and their ears heavy,
>> and blind their eyes;
> lest they see with their eyes,
>> and hear with their ears,
>> and understand with their hearts,
>> and turn and be healed.

(See also Deuteronomy 29:4, Isaiah 44:18, and Jeremiah 5:21 for similar references to eyes, ears, and the message of God.)

[The Reader Has 'Inside' Information]

Here it is easy to slide past the larger point of Jesus. He clearly knew the difference between "you" and "those outside." He did not intend his parables to be easy illustrations of small or trivial truths. His intention was that those who were on the inside should have greater discernment, and gain greater understanding, and stretch themselves to grasp things that would take them both higher in their experience of God and deeper in assurance.

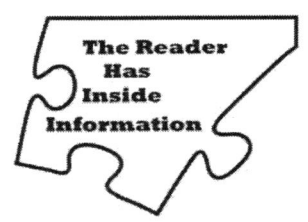

Who are the people included in these two groups -- "you," and "those outside?" When I began my writing on this Gospel account, I felt strongly that I was to include all my readers in the "inside" group. You probably noticed that at the time of Jesus' baptism --

after he came up out of the water he saw the heavens opened and the Spirit descending upon him like a dove; and a voice came from heaven, "You are my beloved Son; with you I am well-pleased."

These are things that Jesus saw and heard, whether or not any bystanders saw them or heard them -- including John the Baptist. But the reader, too, gets to see what Jesus saw, and hear what he heard. We who follow Jesus are on the inside then, getting insider information right from the very start of his mission, and people who are not following him are "those outside."

This distinction is made even clearer in his *interpretation* of the parable of the sower. There are four kinds of soil, but only one kind of seed. The goal of the sowing is the growth of the grain to maturity, the time of bearing much fruit, but there are three kinds of outsiders that will never bear fruit: those who are open to the work of Satan, those who do not have the determination to endure tribulation and persecution, and those who are easily influenced by the cares of the world, who covet riches, or who are enticed by the desire for other things.

So Jesus has divided hearers into four kinds. His description of them leaves only one desired outcome. To grow into maturity is to be in agreement with the will of the Sower, to put trust (that's *faith*) in the sower.

Questioner: Mark, I think I see something I never saw before. In the explanation of the parable it is easier now for us to understand Jesus' division of his hearers into groups. "Those inside" are the fourth group, growing to maturity and bearing fruit. Those who are most obviously *outside* are the first group, where the soil of the mind is hard, and Satan comes and takes away the word from them.

Staying with this parable, the rocky soil and the thorny place both remind us that it is possible to be eager hearers at first but then to become withered or fruitless. The parable clearly is a warning to everyone who wants to be numbered among those on the inside.

Mark: Jesus recognized that not everyone would perceive the meaning of his parables, and with a quotation from Isaiah he said that those outside would hear but not understand. But then the disciples asked him for an interpretation, admitting that they too were not fully "on the inside."

Jesus followed with three other parables: the Lamp-stand, the Seed that Grows by Itself, and the Mustard Seed.

LANDMARK 5

Miracles

Mark continues:
Following the short series of parables you'll remember that there is a matching set of four miracles putting in the spotlight Jesus' power. There is one of each kind: power over *nature*, power over *demons or evil forces*, power over *physical illness*, and power over *death*. (4:35-5:43)

LANDMARK 6.

Great Events, Great Opposition

Next there is a series of events that show the energetic presentation of good news by Jesus and his disciples, a presentation met with mixed results. Jesus was amazed when he was not received in faith by the people of his home town, and his power to perform miracles was limited by their lack of faith. When he sent out the twelve in pairs their ministry was preaching, casting out demons, and anointing for healing. In this case, the presentation and mission seems highly successful.

When Jesus and the disciples attempted to withdraw for a rest they were spotted and sought by thousands, who listened eagerly to Jesus' teaching. Because of his extended time of teaching he also was unwilling to send the thousands of listeners on the long journey toward their homes without food; so, miraculously, he fed the five thousand.

After the feeding, Jesus sent his disciples away across the lake while he withdrew up onto the mountain to pray. Later, when the disciples ran into headwinds Jesus walked on the water -- as far as anyone knows this was the only time he did so -- and then he got into the boat with them.

LANDMARK 7 [chapters 7 & 8]

The Jewish-Gentile Question

Mark continues: Up to this point you could follow the "landmark" idea by identifying each one as about the same as a chapter. This section will be two chapters long, and so will "landmark 8."

In this section Jesus clears up many questions about the Jewish traditions including kosher food laws, purity, symbolic washings, and especially the acceptance of Gentiles.

This becomes an especially important truth for Jesus in chapter 8, where for a second time Jesus feeds thousands of people with very few provisions. This miracle is very similar to his feeding the 5,000, but this time the location is not in Jewish territory, and undoubtedly includes many Gentiles.

LANDMARK 8 [chapters 9 & 10]

The Mission to Followers and Families

Continuing to watch for landmarks in this Gospel, these chapters highlight Jesus' glory and power with his transfiguration and the miraculous cure of a boy who had an unclean spirit that had made him both deaf and mute. In both of these chapters Jesus startles the disciples with predictions of his coming mistreatment and death.

Late in this section the Lord addresses the topics of divorce, the importance God places on children, and the difficulty that the wealthy will have in keeping the Kingdom of God in its rightful place.

THE FINAL LANDMARK   [chapters 11-16]

The Final Week

In this overview I can gather the last six chapters together, for several reasons. First, they represent the events and teachings of just one week. Second, they actually are put together with calendar notations, so the careful reader always knows when a new day has come. And third, they carry a dramatic impact when read through in sequence.

Day one: *Sunday* -- Jesus is acclaimed as he rides into Jerusalem on a borrowed colt. After he looked around he went out to Bethany for lodging. (11:1-11)

Day two: *Monday* --Cursed a fig tree and cleared the Temple of moneychangers and other commercialism. (11:12-19)

Day three: *Tuesday* -- Jesus has questions to answer, from groups that have special interests to defend. The questions relate to authority, submission to Rome, the resurrection, and the greatest commandment of the law. In addition, on this day Jesus taught at some length about the coming destruction of Jerusalem, tied in with the tribulations at the end of time when the Son of Man will return. (11:20-13:37)

Day four: *Wednesday* -- Jesus was anointed as he reclined at the table in the house of Simon the leper in Bethany. Jesus and eleven of the disciples stayed away from Jerusalem on this day, though it was only about two miles from Bethany to Jerusalem. One of the disciples did go into Jerusalem: Judas, the betrayer. (14:1-11)

Day five: *Thursday* -- The Last Supper, Gethsemane, arrest, trial before the High Priest and the Sanhedrin, Peter's denial. (14:12-72)

Day six: *Friday* -- Jesus' trial before Pilate, he is crucified, he breathes his last, then he is laid in a tomb and the entrance was securely sealed. (15:1-47)

Day seven: *Saturday* -- The Sabbath. It is a day of silence, except that after sunset, when the Sabbath was past, (Saturday night), Mary Magdalene, Mary the mother of James, and Salome bought spices to anoint his body early the next day.

Day eight: *Easter Sunday* -- the Day of Resurrection. The women went to the tomb early in the morning, and found the entrance clear and the tomb empty. An angel (called "a young man") told them that they should go and tell his disciples *and Peter* that he is risen!

Questioner: Looking back on your brisk trip through these chapters, it is easier to see how each part fits. As a whole, your Gospel always points us to the best answer for the big question: it was the question that the disciples voiced, and the crowds kept wondering about -- "Who is He?"

Chapter 17

A Series of Final Questions and Issues

Most of the issues (and puzzles) in this chapter have been touched on in one place or another in the earlier parts of the book, but only lightly. So it seemed good to Mark and me that a bit more thought might be a good idea. Here is a list of them.

1 Foreshadowing Jesus' death
2 The Key Verses and Memorable Sayings
3 Style: "Like a Stage Play"
4 The Secrecy Theme
5 Can We Tell How Long Jesus' Ministry Was?
6 Why So Little of Jesus' Teachings?
7 The Over-arching Theme: Who Is He?

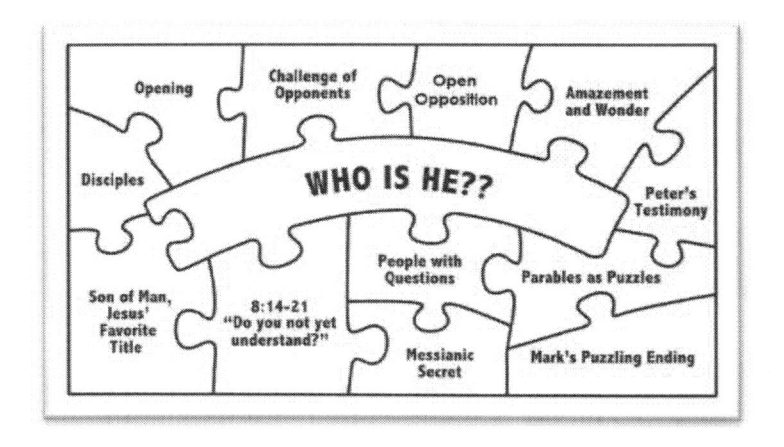

1. Foreshadowing Jesus' Death:

Questioner: Mark, at irregular intervals your writing briefly puts Jesus' coming death into a spotlight. Sometimes they are in the words of Jesus, and sometimes in your comments as the narrator. The most striking of these is the first one, in 3:6, where after Jesus healed the man's withered hand on the Sabbath. "And the Pharisees went out and held counsel with the Herodians, how to destroy him."

Everyone is clear that your writing is not organized in strict chronological order, but I was wondering, do these represent their actual timing in the ministry of Jesus? That is, was it *so very early* in Jesus' mission that the people in power had already put his destruction on their agenda?

Mark: Hm-m-m-m. Your question is interesting, especially because you're inquiring about the opposition of certain groups and also about chronology and timing in my Gospel.

When Jesus began his mission it didn't take long for the leading groups of Jews to put him to the test. They saw their role as being "gatekeepers," whose approval was essential. They wanted to see whether he fit in their picture of Israel and God's plan for the nation.

Because of his claims, forgiving sins (2:10) and lordship over the Sabbath (2:28), he failed their test. Then the next time he healed on the Sabbath they decided to act, because in their minds he was an obstacle to the plan of God. Though Pharisees and Herodians were not natural allies and agreed on very few things, they agreed together to oppose him, and even to form a plot to bring about his destruction.

Even though chronological order is not the most important consideration in my writing, you may see that there is no reason to doubt that serious opposition began very early.

2. Key Verses and Memorable Sayings of Jesus

Questioner: Mark, as you wrote, did you realize how significant the *Key Verse* Was?

Mark: By 'key verse' you probably mean those tremendous words of Jesus.

> *for even the son of man did not come to be served, but to serve and to give his life for many.* (10:45)

We have touched on that earlier, but you're right, it is such an important idea for us to understand that it's good to come back to it.

It's easy to see that this saying is powerful and important. It focuses our attention on Jesus' purpose and goal.

It has always been true that for any great teacher there are certain sayings that live on. This is very true for prophets such as Moses, Jeremiah, and Isaiah; and it is even more true for Jesus. This saying is among the greatest in human history. From the first time I heard Peter quote these words it's as though they were burned into my mind. *The mission of Jesus was not to come and do spectacular things to gain prominence, fame, or power*. He didn't come for himself, he came for others. These words clear that up -- the focus is on his serving others, and ransoming the lives, and even the souls, of others from the power of the evil one.

But, you know, there are also a few other sayings of Jesus that could qualify also as 'key' verses. When he said, *"Render to Caesar the things that are Caesar's, and to God the things that are God's,"* we need to remember that he wasn't only talking about taxes. He would include the moments and days of life.

Here are a few more memorable sayings from Jesus.

• "With man it is impossible, but not with God. For with God all things are possible." (10:27)

• "Is not this why you are wrong, because you know neither the Scriptures nor the power of God?" (12:24)

• "Whoever receives one such child in my name receives me, and whoever receives me receives not me but him who sent me." (9:37)

• "He that is not against us is for us." (9:40)

• "Do not fear: only believe." (5:36b)

3. Like a Stage Play?

Questioner: Your account contains a lot of information about Jesus that helps us to feel that we're getting to know Jesus. In fact, you've written in a narrative style that in some places seems almost like a drama written for the stage. In each scene you have a cast of characters, and there is action described, and much additional information is carried through dialogue.

We're all aware that the Greek-speaking world passed along much of its important information through drama, not only with the formal plays, but, according to some scholars, even the writing of philosophy. Some of them speculate that the Dialogues of Plato may have been written to be performed on the stage. So my question to you, Mark, is this: did you write with the idea that your account of the Gospel could be produced onstage?

Mark: It's interesting that you would ask this question. I haven't heard that one before. And frankly, my short answer is "no." I didn't have that in mind.

But I have a longer answer, too. Now that you mention it, I can see that many parts of this account of the Good News could be adapted for performance before an audience. In fact, understanding some of the encounters of opponents with Jesus might spring even more vividly to the mind of a live audience than it does to readers. I'm not saying that the written Word of God is not powerful, nor that it should have been written as a theater piece. But what I can say is that just as it is, it has sufficient power that it can find many applications.

I say this not because I think of myself as a good writer, but because my writing centers on Christ. So at the center of everything is the power in Jesus himself.

4. The 'Secrecy' Theme

Questioner: Mark, many people have noticed the number of times in your description of Jesus' activities when he heals someone or otherwise helps them, and then charges them not to tell anyone about it. There are other features that seem to accompany this stealth theme, and to some it seems so prominent that they have even given it a name -- "the messianic secret." Sometimes interpreters even try out the notion that the secrecy idea comes not from Jesus, but from you as the writer. Could you give us some additional insight about this?

Mark: There is a bit of a story here -- it's true that often Jesus tried to keep a low profile. Sometimes that wasn't possible, but one time after another he commanded persons to keep silent after a bold miraculous work:

> "See that you say nothing to anyone..." (1:44)
> "... he strictly charged them that no one should know this ..." (5:43)
> "Jesus charged them to tell no one. But the more he charged them the more zealously they proclaimed it." (7:36)
> "And he sent him to his home, saying, 'Do not even enter the village.'" (8:26)

Questioner: Yes, a lot of people have noticed that. And even with his disciples Jesus cautioned them not to be too open. Maybe instead of *secrecy* we should call it "confidentiality." Immediately following the momentous witness of Peter, "You are the Christ," come your words,

> "And he strictly charged them to tell no one about him" (8:30).

And in a similar way, when unclean spirits cried out in recognition of him Jesus also commanded their silence (1:25, 34; 3:12). One difference is that it appears that the demons by necessity had to obey him, but the people didn't, for "the more he charged them the more strongly they proclaimed it." (7:36)

Why would Jesus *not* want publicity?

Most people wonder why Jesus would counsel silence, or even command it, instead of welcoming publicity. Even the brothers of Jesus on one occasion told Jesus to go to the most public place he could, because "no one works in secret if he seeks to be known openly. If you do these things show yourself to the world."

Mark: You or I might wonder about this secrecy -- but if we think about it for a while, some answers pop up.
> 1. *Jesus already had as much popularity as it was possible for him to still continue his mission.*
>
>   Here's an example: after being healed, the leper "... went out and began to talk freely about it, and to spread the news, so that Jesus could no longer openly enter a town...." (1:45)

Some time later Jesus came back to Capernaum,

> "and many were gathered together, so that there was no more room, not even at the door and he was preaching the word to them." (2:2)

Here are other examples:
> "Jesus withdrew with his disciples to the sea, and a great crowd followed, from Galilee and Judea and Jerusalem and Idumea and from beyond the Jordan and from around Tyre and Sidon. When the great crowd heard all that he was doing, they came to him." (3:7-8)

> "And he told his disciples to have a boat ready for him because of the crowd, lest they crush him ...." (3:9)

"... for he had healed many, so that all who had diseases pressed around him to touch him." (3:10)

"Again he began to teach beside the sea. And a very large crowd gathered about him, so that he got into a boat and sat in it on the sea, and the whole crowd was beside the sea on the land." (4:1)

So with crowds like these, it would be strange to suggest that Jesus needed more publicity.

2. But on the other hand, knowing a bit about human nature we know that there are times when we can count on people to do just what we ask them *not* to do.

Jesus healed a leper and made a request, "see that you say nothing to anyone" (except the priests, who had the responsibility of granting or refusing him a clean bill of health). But he couldn't keep the healing to himself, and went around speaking freely about it. (1:40-45)

When the man who was deaf and had speech difficulty was healed of both, Jesus charged the people near him to tell no one about it, "but the more he charged them the more zealously they proclaimed it." (7:36)

If this seems to be a stretch -- to suggest that Jesus directly asked people <u>not</u> to do precisely what he wanted them to do -- then drop that idea.

Questioner: But I see that it may help us all to see that lack of information about Jesus was never a problem. In fact, when we take that into account it brings us to the most important reason for the "confidentiality" theme.

3. Jesus was the Messiah, but the popular idea of a messiah was distorted and incomplete. Even if every fragment of the popular portrait of the messiah came directly from the Old Testament, its predictions and promises, a full portrait is hard to see. Some parts of the scriptures had reference to an ideal leader walking in great obedience to God, embodying the goals and aspirations of the nation, and described as a leader of the nation, a king or a prince.

Mark: Some of the Old Testament references were obvious predictions of an actual person; but others seemed to many people like descriptions of an ideal man, almost like saying "what if there could be someone like this." Some passages referred to a warrior-king, destroying the nation's enemies with great bravery and skill. Some describe him reigning over Israel -- and his reign will go far beyond Israel, to bring peace over vast regions of the earth. But others picture him meek and lowly; and still others as a judge and final moral authority.

Now this varied picture of the leader of Israel came to be tied to the term Messiah, *Anointed*. Over many generations, the times between the end of the writings of the prophets and the time of fulfillment, when Jesus came, there were three centuries or more in which the imagination of the teachers and the common people expanded the picture greatly. Isaiah the prophet, for example, had written, "... *of the increase of his government and peace there will be no end upon the throne of David and over his kingdom ...*" (Isaiah 9:7)

Questioner: Such words seem to beg for further explanation, don't they? So scenarios developed of what this peace would be like. The commonly accepted view included not only peace, but also the one feature that seems most often to be necessary to bring and maintain peace -- and that is power, specifically military power. Even the twelve disciples held this view, and expressed it often. [See 10:35-37, Acts 1:6]

For this reason the accepted portrait of the messiah, in the view of common people and leaders alike, came to include military skills and forceful governance as well as international respect -- or fear.

With expectations like these, how well prepared were the people of Galilee and Judea to recognize and accept the messiah who comes as the courageous yet humble *servant of the Lord*?

> There are four famous 'servant songs' in Isaiah, with application both to Israel's experience and to the coming messiah. See Isaiah 42:1-4, where his humility is the

215

emphasis, and Isaiah 49:1-6, where the focus is on the <u>power of his message</u>, combined with a measure of <u>discouragement</u> and <u>rejection</u>, and the enlargement of his mission to become "a light for the nations." The last of these songs is the most dramatic messianic prophecy of all, with the explicit statement "All we, like sheep, have gone astray; and the Lord has laid on him the iniquity of us all." Isaiah 53:6

Mark: All of the servant passages in Isaiah could have the words "suffering servant" attached to them, for in each one there is the description of mistreatment, rejection, or outright abuse of the servant of the Lord. And in each of them there is one or more elements of the life of Jesus, the messiah.

Questioner: Looking back, and seeing the Old Testament prophecies about the messiah, we can see how clearly they describe Jesus and his mission. However, there are a number of them that have not yet matched up. Jesus tried to give us clarity on that, too. When we look at the many things that Jesus said about God's plan for the future, or what we may call the 'end times,' we can see that there are two very different aspects to his mission. They can be distinguished in these ways:

Now in the past	Still in the future
Earthly servant	Triumphant Lord

At the risk of making it too simple, I'll just say that when he came the first time as the teacher from Galilee, he spoke the truth from God, but he was opposed by powerful people, and he was killed. Jesus himself put it in brief and memorable terms (10:45):

> **The Son of Man did not come to be Served, but to Serve, and to give his Life as a Ransom for Many**

We've looked at this at least twice before, of course, because for many people this stands out as the *most important verse* of my account of the Gospel. It may not be a coincidence that he used the term *serve*, which may remind us of the *servant* of the Lord.

So there are these three reasons why Jesus cautioned people not to be his publicity agents.

1) He already had huge crowds, and could not readily handle more.

2) He knew some people would tell all the more, despite his warning.

3) The people of Israel had certain preconceived notions about a messiah that didn't allow for the earthly and suffering servant part of his mission.

5. Can We Tell How Long Jesus' Ministry Lasted?

Questioner: Your Gospel account seems to move along very fast, and with a breathless quality. It's hard to get any sense of the passage of time as we read. We often hear that the public ministry of Jesus lasted three or three and one-half years, but from your writing it would be hard to figure that out. Why can't we tell how much time any part of the Gospel represents?

Mark: Well, yes, I can see why you would ask that. But if you look at chapter one alone, you'll see that I embedded a few clues for you to keep in mind. Jesus taught in the synagogue in Capernaum, and while still in the same synagogue he cast an unclean spirit out of a man.

> "And they were all amazed, so that they questioned among themselves, saying, 'What is this? A new teaching with authority! He commands even the unclean spirits, and they obey him.' And at once his fame spread throughout all the surrounding region of Galilee. And immediately he left the synagogue and entered the house of Simon and Andrew...." (1:27-29)

You noticed, didn't you, that I noted that *at once his fame spread* throughout Galilee, even before I mentioned his leaving the synagogue? In our days, well before your electronic methods of communication and social media, this wouldn't have happened so instantly. But I included this knowing that alert readers would see that for me, strict chronological order was not high on my list of priorities. (You can see, can't you, that I proceeded from *landmark to landmark*, or theme to theme -- for example, beginning with wide acceptance, then challenges, opposition, parables, miracles, and so on.)

But back to that first section. After healing Simon's mother-in-law and then curing many people that evening, just a bit later I wrote of a ministry tour "throughout all Galilee" in just one sentence:

> And he went throughout all Galilee, preaching in their synagogues and casting out demons. (1:39)

The tour itself, preaching in the synagogues of most or all of the towns in Galilee along with other incidental ministry, would have taken quite an extension of time, perhaps four to eight months. But I didn't go into any detail on the preaching because I prepared the reader by giving the essential content of the message in four easy parts earlier in the chapter (1:14-15), and I gave a sample of information about his typical encounters with demons also. (1:23-26; 1:34)

The point is that many times I gave a very brief summary of things that happened over a longer period of time. As you read, watch for the clues. As for just *how long* the time of his ministry lasted, may I defer that question, or not give you an easy answer. In fact, I hope that question can fade away: and I hope this won't sound too simple. The ministry of Christ isn't finished yet. He isn't in the tomb; he is alive. My real purpose is to bring you and all my readers, whenever you pick up my Gospel, into the presence of Christ.

As Isaiah the prophet wrote, "in a time of favor I have answered you; in a day of salvation I have helped you." I believe that the moment Jesus becomes real in our minds becomes a day of salvation. I hope you will not use my Gospel as *history*, but as a discovery of Christ. I want to invite you into his world, and into his presence.

6. Why does it seem like we have so little of Jesus' words and of his teaching in this Gospel?

Questioner: Many people notice that in your Gospel there aren't many passages presenting extended teachings of Jesus. Only in chapter 13, where he predicts some seriously troubled times ahead, do we see so much of Jesus' teaching. Aside from that, quotations of Jesus are only in short sayings, usually as a response to a request, a question, or an event. Why does this seem to be the case?

Mark: Actually, there are 661 verses in the Gospel that I wrote. You will find Jesus speaking in over 275 of them, or something like 42% of the verses. Doesn't that seem like a pretty good proportion? You may have expected some long sermons or teaching occasions like the Sermon on the Mount or the "missionary discourse." Other gospel accounts include those lengthy teaching occasions, and we can all be glad they do.

The *first* purpose of my writing was to present Jesus, the Christ, the Son of God for the people of Rome, the ones Peter and I gave witness to. I wanted my writing to speak to them and help them to learn and grow in their understanding of the Lord. I wasn't even aware of a *second* purpose, but soon some people made a copy and took it to other places, to share the word. Eventually, other copies were made, and the rest is history.

No one yet thought of this information as *scripture*. That would come many years later. Somehow, though, it proved helpful enough over a large enough region so that much, much later, it was included along with other writings as part of the Bible.

My Gospel is not more important than the others, because in fact each one has its place. It is pretty certain that when you read this document you can get a sense of Jesus in his mission of salvation. He gave his life as a ransom for us.

7. The Over-arching Theme: Who Is He?

WHO IS HE??

Questioner: I see clearly that the main question always in mind in your Gospel account is the question "*Who Is He?*" It's a question that could be asked in every chapter -- and sometimes was voiced in just that way by the people around Jesus. You gave a detailed answer earlier, but before we part, could you give me a short review of the answer?

Mark: Sure. The answer has several parts, so how about a list? All of these have already come up in our conversations, so if I merely list them, with a brief description, it should be a good reminder.

> 1. Son of Man: *Three parts, drawn from Old Testament thought: Authoritative, Suffering, and Apocalyptic (that is, Coming Again, as in Daniel 7:14).* Each one of these is very important if we want understanding, or to know Jesus better.
>
> 2. Son of God: *Spoken by God, demons, Jesus himself, the centurion at the cross, and --what I wrote in the first verse ('Jesus Christ, Son of God').*
>
> 3. Christ: *this title is not found often, but it's highly important wherever it*

appears. (See especially 8:29, Peter's very important testimony, and 1:1 again)

4. The Servant: *who gives up his life as a ransom for many.* (10:45)

5. *The things he did and the things he said* declare who he is, even more than the names or titles. He commanded the winds and the sea (4:39-41); he commanded demons (1:27); he forgave sins and proved it with an accompanying sign (2:5-12); he knew ahead of time he was to suffer and die, and he went to the cross willingly, a ransom for others.

Puzzling things in Mark
-- Some things from each chapter of the Gospel

Chapter 1:

- Where did Jesus come from? What was his background?

- Why did (and why *would*) the first four disciples abruptly leave their fishing business and follow Jesus?

- How long did it take for the events of chapter one to take place?

Chapter 2:

- How did Jesus know what the scribes were thinking in their hearts?

- It seems to be written as no surprise to anyone in the story that a group of men tore apart part of the roof of a house in order to bring a paralyzed man to Jesus. Really, they weren't surprised??

- There is no explanation why Levi left his tax table. Were there assistants who were trusted to carry on the responsibilities?

- Customs and rules are not explained. For example, why was plucking heads of grain on the Sabbath day forbidden?

Chapter 3:

- It seems puzzling to read that the groups that were fierce rivals of each other got together and agreed in a plan to destroy Jesus.

- One group that opposed Jesus seems vague and puzzling: literally, "those who had been with him." Neighbors? Friends? Family? Early disciples who had abandoned him? Maybe boys who had grown up with him? And-- why exactly do they think that he is crazy?

Chapter 4:

- Why does it seem to us that Jesus does *not* want those outside to understand, "...and be forgiven"?

- What is the meaning of the parable of the Seed Growing on its Own?

- Why are we prepared to see many parables here but find far fewer?

- Why, after following Jesus for many months, do the disciples ask "who then is this...?"

Chapter 5:

- Why did 2,000 pigs have to die to rid the man of a legion of demons?

- How did it feel for power to go out of Jesus?

Chapter 6:

- In numerous places Jesus responds in power to the faith that people express. Here he "could do no mighty work." He was the Son of God: why was he so limited in his own home town?
- When walking on the water, why did he intend to pass by them?

Chapter 7:

- This chapter is pretty free of puzzles and puzzling things; but most translations get it a bit wrong when they quote Jesus as saying "let the children be fed first, because it is not a good thing to take the children's food and pitch it to the dogs." Gentiles are *dogs*?? Not really -- the word Jesus used is "puppies," and it makes a huge difference.

Chapter 8:

- Why does Jesus use *more* loaves to feed *fewer* people, and have *less* food left over?

- Why does Jesus go so far as to call Peter *Satan*?

Chapter 9:

- What is the significance of the Transfiguration of Jesus?

- Why, after being taught by Jesus for such a long time, did the disciples dispute over who was the greatest?

Chapter 10:

- Why did James and John want to be seated, one on Jesus' right and the other on his left, [when Jesus is]in his glory?

Chapter 11:

- Why did Jesus seem to have no plan or agenda for the rest of Palm Sunday after he entered Jerusalem?

- Why did he curse the fig tree, since it was not the season for figs?

- When they saw that the tree had suddenly died, why did Jesus teach on faith and prayer, instead of giving a warning about judgment to come?

Chapter 12:

- What does it mean to be "not far from the Kingdom of God"?

- Why did Jesus *let* the widow put into the temple treasury all she had to live on?

Chapter 13:

- Among all the puzzling things about the end of the world, why is it that the Son of God did not know when it will happen?

Chapter 14:

- Why is it that Jesus knew who the betrayer was, and did not ask the other disciples to keep him away?

- Why does this Gospel include the strange little incident of a young man who was almost seized, but who slipped out of the cloth he had wrapped himself in and fled away naked? No other Gospel includes it.

Chapter 15:

- Simon the man from Cyrene is introduced as the father of Alexander and Rufus, but who are *they*? It seems as though these sons must have been well known to the earliest readers of Mark's Gospel.

- This chapter has less of a "puzzling" nature than anywhere else in Mark, but it is filled with vivid descriptions and events that both amaze us and fill us with awe.

Chapter 16:

- If Mark ended his writing with 16:8, this is his best puzzle. He forces us as interested readers to draw our own conclusions about the continuation of the story. We can't leave it there, but we have all the information we need to fill in the blanks. He *was* raised from the dead. Death is not what it seems. (Remember 5:39, where Jesus says, "Why are you weeping and making a commotion? The child is not dead but sleeping.") And who would know the truth about death and the life in its next dimension better than Jesus?

- You may have noticed that there are a few unanswered questions, a few puzzles, in this book, too. I haven't attempted to give solutions to all of Mark's puzzles, but to call attention to his technique, a technique that the Spirit of God endorsed when He directed devout believers to include the earliest, shortest, and most puzzling of the Gospels in the Canon of Scripture. The puzzles are there to engage our minds in the process of loving God with heart, soul, *mind*, and strength. (12:30)

Made in the USA
Lexington, KY
16 April 2014